READING
WITH
DEEPER
EYES

READING WITH
DEEPER EYES

*The Love
of Literature
and the Life of Faith*

WILLIAM H. WILLIMON

UPPER
ROOM BOOKS
NASHVILLE

Cover Transparency: © DigitalVision
Cover Design: Gore Studio, Inc.
First Printing 1998

The Upper Room Web Site: http://www.upperroom.org

The Library of Congress Cataloging-in-Publication Data

Willimon, William H.
    Reading with deeper eyes: the love of literature and the life of faith / William H. Willimon.
        p. cm.
    Includes bibliographical references.
    ISBN 0-8358-0847-5
    1. Christian life—Methodist authors. 2. Christianity and literature. I. Title.
    BV4501.2.W5445   1998
    261.5'8—DC21   97-26043
                                                                        CIP

Printed in the United States of America

TO STANLEY HAUERWAS

CONTENTS

"WHENEVER, therefore, we meet with heathen writers, let us learn from that light of truth which is admirably displayed in their works, that the human mind, fallen as it is, and corrupted from its integrity, is yet invested and adorned by God with excellent talents. If we believe that the Spirit of God is the only fountain of truth, we shall neither reject nor despise the truth itself, wherever it shall appear, unless we wish to insult the Spirit of God."

—John Calvin

The Love of Literature
and the Life of Faith

No Christian prays or believes or acts alone. Fortunately, God has not left us to our own devices. We are formed by the saints—those who came before us. We are not the first to tackle the challenges of discipleship. Others have walked this way. Some built churches to witness to their faith. Others painted pictures. Most of them lived like us—quiet, rather uneventful but nevertheless faithful lives, feeding the hungry, loving the poor, pouring over the scriptures, trying to be the church in their time—then they went to be with God, remembered only by their Creator who took delight in their fidelity.

I am here most interested in those saints who have told us what they knew through literature. Most good writers do not like to be called teachers, but they are. Although didacticism is the death of good writing, Augustine said that all good communication not only delights but also teaches. To teach is to delight. Each of us, when we read a book, looks over someone's shoulder, trying to figure out the other, hoping to see what another sees, grubbing for a clue as to what is going on in the world, delighting in the experience of living through someone else's life, if just for a few hours. The philosopher, and sometime novelist, Iris Murdoch once called good art "a kind of goodness by proxy." Through another's art, we get to try on another's being, get to look at the world through another's eyes, which aids our moral imagination, which leads to good.

I have found that most good writers do not like to be called "Christian writers." This is not only because some artists have problems with what they think they know of Christianity. Many good writers are "loners" who do most of their work in quiet seclusion, whereas Christianity is a decidedly group thing where we do most of our work together. Good novelists are noted for their relentless honesty, whereas, the church is often noted for its pretense and hypocrisy. "Christian writer" gives off more than a whiff of tedious moralizing, scolding, or else fluffy, ethereal musings on spiritual things with all the substance of a bowl of sweet meringue. Say "spiritual" more than a dozen times and you will find yourself floating a few feet above ground. Most good writers cling closely to the solid stuff of earth.

However, art, good art, is an effort to render the world truthfully, to bring to speech that which is often left unspoken because it is too painful, or too wonderful, or too beyond the range of most of our pitiful powers of description. Sometimes a writer, in her determined attempt to tell what she knows, just can't help telling about God—the constricted, skeptical literary establishment be damned. Sometimes, despite themselves, God gives writers the slip and pops up in a story, even when the author thought that this story had no room for God. God loves to do that.

At other times, through story, the human condition is rendered so honestly that, even though God is not explicitly mentioned in the story, the questions which the story raises, the life dilemmas with which it deals make necessary a God who loves and redeems or else we are utterly without hope.

As a preacher I am (as Augustine described himself) a "word merchant." Words are the only tools in my ministerial bag of tricks. So I have a vested interest in the writers' use, and my frequent abuse, of language. I'm always on the prowl for help in bringing the gospel of Jesus Christ to speech, and I am not too proud to receive aid from an allegedly pagan writer. John Wesley, who read nearly everyone of his day without discrimination, called this "plundering the Egyptians."

Yet when you think about it, you also are a peddler of language. Words are all any of us have to make sense of this world. When God began creating the world, according to Genesis, God did it through speech. Creation is a story which begins with the silence being broken by, "And God said . . ." When Jesus burst upon the scene, Mark had to invent a new literary device, something he called "gospel," because no available means could carry the freight. Nor is it mere happenstance that when Jesus taught, he taught mostly through story, parable being the uniquely Jesus way of talking to people about the salvation of God.

None of us can live without story. Nobel Prize winner Sir Peter Medawar says that even scientists go about their work by "telling stories which are scrupulously tested to see if they are stories about real life." For each of us, life is a long process of testing which stories are true, which stories are worth living for and dying by.

This book is my attempt to share my love for and debt to the writing of others in my own struggling discipleship. I begin with, of all people, an ancient Greek poet named Homer, and compare his account of the search for home with a story told by Jesus. Two chapters later we sit on life's ash heap with brother Job, demanding to see God, then being shocked by the God we see. The dark questions of Job seem a perfect prelude to Dostoyevsky's somber vision of sin and its consequence, salvation and its cost. We then jump forward to more contemporary explorations of the divine in Oscar Hijuelos and Flannery O'Connor. Each sees the modern world not as a flat, secular, godless machine but rather as creation bursting at the seams with revelation. They prepare us for less positive assessments of God's way with the modern world as found in Walker Percy, John Updike, and Peter De Vries. If we are to be lured back to God, these contemporaries imply, the way back will not be easy. Anne Tyler wonderfully depicts the glory within the ordinary, the power of a life lived in ordinary fidelity to the way of Christ. Finally, in a much more mystical way, Ron Hansen renders a world where God is lurking and, despite our best secular defenses, may have us yet.

When I walk with Jesus, a considerable crowd of unlikely saints walk with me, giving me encouragement for the journey, an invitation to join in a conversation which began long before we were born and shall continue long after we are dead—God rendered through literature, ancient and modern, God with us as the Word made flesh, then made words so that we might be the Word enfleshed again.

1

The Way
Back Home

The Odyssey

> But we had to celebrate and rejoice, because this brother
> of yours was dead and has come to life; he was lost and
> has been found.
> —Luke 15:32

When I was a freshman at Wofford College, I read the *Odyssey* our first semester. I expect that most of us read it with bafflement. What had such an old story to do with us? I am sure that our professor told us that all Western literature has its genesis in this epic by the West's first epic poet. We know next to nothing about Homer, where he came from or who he was. Yet we are his numberless heirs. Behind the adventures and exploits of Odysseus, Homer's hero of the Trojan war, lie countless other plots and subplots used repeatedly by tellers of tales down through the ages.

The *Odyssey* is an old story in every sense of the term. It is more than 2,500 years old. Not as old, therefore, as most of the Bible, but old nevertheless. Despite its age, the *Odyssey* still speaks to us because it is humanity's same old story, a faithful rendering of the human situation which still is able to speak because of its faithfulness.

Yet to characterize the *Odyssey* in this way is to imply that all a writer does is to describe reality faithfully, simply give us a picture of what is already there. In a deep sense, there is no "there" until the story tells about what is there. Our stories, like the *Odyssey,* don't just report on what has been or is, rather they create something which would not be there without the story. Our words don't just *describe* the world, they *make* the world.

It is a wonderful, threatening, conflicted world which is rendered by the *Odyssey.* As the story opens, all the survivors of the Trojan War have returned home—except for Odysseus. The gods have made mischief for our hero—the nymph Calypso wants him for her husband, and Poseidon, ruler of the sea, has a grudge against him and wants to make his way home as rough as possible. This is the way the world works in Homer. We humans are mere playthings of the gods. According to this Greek perspective, we live in a world which is unpredictable and confusing because the gods are forever squabbling and wreaking havoc with our plans. We can either resign ourselves to the absurdity of it all or, like Odysseus, heroically wrestle with the gods, sometimes tricking them into serving us rather than our being servile to them. Odysseus is the first of literature's great heroes, the prototype for all who were to follow. The heroes were those who dealt with the world by being as much like the gods as a human could and thus carved out for themselves some shred of human dignity amid a world where the gods cared little for us or our welfare.

The gods have a council and, through the pleading of Athene, Zeus decides to call off the gods' affliction of Odysseus. Athene disguises herself and goes to the home of Odysseus. There, Odysseus' son, Telemachus, and his wife, Penelope, have endured the indignity of having their home overrun by a horde of suitors. They are not only attempting to court Penelope but they are wasting all of Odysseus' property with their banquets and feasts.

Athene, disguising herself as old Mentes, an old friend of Odysseus, is welcomed by Telemachus. The two sit down to dinner and Telemachus apologizes for the crudeness of all the suitors. Telemachus asks for news of his father and is reassured by Mentes (who is really Athene) that Odysseus is alive, even now making his way toward home.

In rather whining tones, Telemachus laments his present situation. He is a virtual prisoner in his own home, powerless to defend his mother or his father's property against the suitors. Mentes (from whose name we get our term "mentor") urges young Telemachus to stand up on his own two feet, to act for once like a man, and put the suitors to rout.

This Telemachus finally does. At Mentes' urging, he stands on his own two feet—which the Greeks defined as the essence of adulthood or wisdom—puts the suitors out of his house, bids farewell to his mother, and sets out to find his long lost father.

The story of Telemachus is a little novel within a novel, occupying most of Books I and IV of the *Odyssey*. This story of the maturation, the mentoring, and the rise to adulthood of the young man has been called by scholars the *Telemacheia*, the story of Telemachus' entry into the adult world.

For the Greeks, and the civilizations they spawned, this became the conventional path to adulthood. Odysseus becomes an adult, a full human being, only by leaving home, deserting wife and family and sailing forth on a "wine dark sea" toward fame and adventure. His son, Telemachus, can only become an adult by a similar path, forsaking a tearful mother and venturing forth in search of his father.

Women appear in the *Odyssey* only as tempters, those who dissuade men from their real mission in life, or as tearful wives or mothers bidding farewell, waiting faithfully at home for their men to return, bringing them some news from the real world which is always somewhere other than at home.

Of course, my freshman year of college was a perfect time to read Homer's story. It really was our story, even though we may at first have failed to recognize ourselves in it. We were, like Odysseus, venturing forth on uncharted seas. We had, like young Telemachus, left parents, neighborhood, and home to seek our fortunes which were somewhere other than at home.

The *Odyssey* is an interesting story, even though it is wrong, not because Homer's story was fiction and therefore not true (for all truth is best encountered through fiction), but because Homer's story was a story about a god other than the God of Israel.

Each of us attempts to make sense out of life through stories. If we can't tell a story about ourselves, then we are nothing more than detached bundles of facts, dates, and faces signifying nothing. Every people makes sense of itself through certain master stories. Ancient Greece listened to Homer's tale of Odysseus who ventured on a wine dark sea. "Here is what life is about. This is who we are and ought to be. Here is how the world looks," they seemed to be saying to themselves.

Jesus told another story of a father and two sons. You find it in Luke 15:11-32. We know the story as "The Prodigal Son," although Jesus doesn't give his stories titles. In Jesus' story, a son left home, traveled to a "distant country," and finally came to his senses and home. In Homer's story, with the father gone, it was the son, Telemachus, who realized that, with his old man away on business for the gods know how long, he must grow up and take charge of things at home. Eventually, the father returns, but not before Telemachus has had to stand on his own two feet.

In Jesus' story, the father waits for the son to come to his senses and back home—which Jesus defined as wisdom. The Greeks wondered what to do when one is abandoned by the father. Jesus, good Jew that he was, pondered life as a problem of never being able to be rid of the father.

In his book *The Parables of Grace*, Robert F. Capon provides a fun way of retelling this parable. For example, the parable begins with the younger son saying, "Father, give me my inheritance." Capons states in other words the son is telling his father to drop dead. (Is there any other way to put the old man's will into effect?) And the old man does just that. Here we see an image of maturation which is most congenial to our society. America was built by slaves, people who were forced to leave home or by immigrants, people who left their parents to seek their fortunes in this "far country" of an allegedly New World. And they in turn taught their children through the Western expansion and the frontier mindset of moving on to new territories that the only way to get anywhere was to emigrate, to leave home, sever parental ties.

I work at a university. There, we get students on campus, detach them from their parents, abandon them to an environment peopled at night exclusively by others their age, tell them to question everything, and once we get them completely cut loose, we call them adult, ready to graduate, to be "on your own," which is what they have been already. The "far country" of the story is the average campus. Everybody is forced to abandon parents in order to grow up.

Why is this the conventional American path to wisdom? IBM needs mobile workers. The multinational corporation requires people who will move at a moment's notice, people who are trained to subordinate family, tradition, friends, values, place to the demands of the company. Rootless, placeless people are more malleable than those who have a home and refuse to leave it. They can be better managed than those who must still answer to the old man.

But back to our story. Out in the "far country" Jesus says the boy engages in "loose living." Loose living invariably appears more interesting in imagination than in reality. Eventually it was hangover, empty pockets, wake up, Monday morning. Do you know someone whose partying is just a little too determined to be real fun? As if one were partying because there was something, someone pulling the strings? "Loose living" is often anything but loose.

And so the boy "comes to himself." He comes back, to himself, saying, "Wait a minute. I don't have to starve out here. I have a father, a home."

And he turns back toward home. He has written a little speech for the occasion. "Dad, er, uh, I mean, Father, I have sinned. I am unworthy to be called your son. Treat me as one of your hired servants."

But the father isn't interested in speeches.

"Chill it, Howard," says the father. "Save the flowery speeches for your application to law school. Come on in. I'll show you a real party."

Which is why this story has always been a shocker. We thought Jesus came to raise ethical standards, to put a bit more muscle into our moral fiber. Here is the homecoming of a ne'er-do-well as a party. It isn't what we expect. We want the father to be gracious, but not overly so. Homecomings for prodigals are fine when dressed in sackcloth and ashes, not in patent leather pumps and a tux. Our question is that of the older brother, "Is it fitting to throw a party for a prodigal?"

What we want is, "Yes, Howard, glad that you're back home. Now let's do away with that left earring and let's have a bit more responsibility out of you. Go in, have a good, balanced meal and then let's talk about finishing your application to law school. OK, Howard?"

No. It's a story about a party, thrown by a father for a prodigal.

Then enters the older brother. Nostrils flared, look of indignation: "Music! Dancing! Levity! and on a Wednesday! What is going on?" he asks the servant.

"Your kid brother's home. The old man has given everybody the night off and there's a party."

He was angry and wouldn't go in. The father comes out into the darkness and begs him to come party.

"Lo these many years have I served you," he sneers to the old man, "turning your turnip business around, putting the books in the black (As Capon notes, he's big on bookkeeping, this older brother) and you never gave me a party."

Chesterton said that there are two ways to get home. One is to go away and come back, the other is never to leave. There is a push and pull inside us, conflict between wanting to go and resenting that we stayed. The story of the Prodigal Son says that there is also a push and pull outside us. God. It is the Father who waits for one to come home and the other to come party. The story begins and ends with the Father.

As Walter Brueggemann notes, the most interesting character in the story is not the prodigal son or the older brother. It's the father. He's the real prodigal, in that his love is extravagant, more excessive than either the younger brother's loose living or the older brother's moral rectitude.

It's a story about a parent who is excessive in his persistence to have a family, an old man who meets us when we drag in from the far country after good times go bad, or who comes out to the lonely dark of our righteousness and begs us to come in and party.

I think that it's a story about you, a story about what it's like to be claimed. The younger brother is well known to us in our families. He is the person who is always gasping for air, threatening to leave, and sometimes leaving. In each of us, there is a person who is gasping, reaching for space, kicking at the bounds.

The older brother is also known to us. He is the always dutiful and thoughtful one, caring, concerned and eventually filled with great resentment. Anybody gets tired of being responsible all the time. Every family has someone who carries so much of the moral weight that after a while he or she just gets tired and feels used and sick of other people not shaping up.

But it's mainly a story about the father. Brueggemann says that finally both sons must deal with the father. On the one hand, he gives both the sons what they need. He lets the younger son come back to the family. The father also gives to the older brother what he needs—reassurance: "You are always with me. Everything I've got is yours" (Luke 15:31, AP).

On the other hand, the father does not give the younger son what he wants: "Make me just one of your hired hands."

"No, I'm not going to do that. You will have to act responsibly." And the older son also wants a party. "No," says the father. "You're not going to get a party. What you're going to get is everything, including your brother."

Atheism once required a kind of intellectual courage. It took a Bertrand Russell or somebody like that to pull it off. Now godlessness is the *modus operandi* of the average American. We are all busy self-actualizing in some far country of self-indulgence or else in some lonely dark of self-righteousness. Yet even in our modern world, our actions betray our parentage. There is something a bit too determined in either our loose living or our righteous indignation, as if we knew that, when our chips are down, the Old Man still awaited us, as if, when the loose living had finally trapped us or our self-righteousness exhausted us, the Old Man would still be there waiting to plead with us, or to forgive us, either way to take us.

The Bible never questions, "Is there a God?" The Bible's question is, "Who is the God who is there?"

The story's claim that God is the parent who refuses to stop silently waiting or earnestly pleading for you collides with modern self-understanding that our lives are our possessions, like a Chevrolet, to do with as we please. We have been initiated into a world of "the individual," an invention of the eighteenth century. We all believe that there is no way to grow up without severing ties, putting parents, values, and community behind. We sever ties with parents only to abandon our young to the most totalitarian group of all, namely, people just like them.

The Prodigal Son construes a world where people have a home, where someone is determined to have us, where younger brothers and sisters leave and resentful older brothers and sisters won't leave.

The Prodigal Son is an assault on some of our culture's most widely held and deeply cherished values, a collision with some of our most popular stories.

The Kantian fiction of the individual as the sole center of meaning has exercised a more powerful influence over our society and its institutions than the story of the Prodigal Son. We are thus victims of the Enlightenment story that we are most fully ourselves when we are most detached from any values other than those we have personally chosen. Little wonder then that homelessness has become the image of our culture, a culture in which intense loneliness is a necessary byproduct of a people determined to be free of all attachments save the most debilitating attachment of all—enslavement to ourselves.

This story of the wayward son who comes home to a party suggests morality begins not in our being free, or thinking "objectively," but in our having a claim laid upon us. "Your brother is home," or, "Son, all that I have is yours."

The story is about the way to true wisdom. Not the conventional modern tale of a journey deeper, ever deeper, into the recesses of your own ego, for that's a way not to grow but to shrink, says the story. Rather, it's a story about two brothers who had a father. Without the father there is no family, no story. The old man loves both boys and is determined to love them in ways that do not abandon them to their own devices.

Conversation overheard last fall on Parent's Weekend. Two women. "Well, your son is twenty-one, is he? It must feel great to be finished with him."

"Are you kidding?" asked the other. "I'll not be finished with him until the day I die." Paradoxically, herein is true freedom, to know who owns you, claims you. I tell students: If you don't know to whom you belong, who it is who awaits you, you're apt to be the willing victim of anybody blowing through town who promises some means of overcoming your sense of emptiness.

When you stand before the powers of the corporation or the conformist pressures of the group, the totalitarian tendencies of modern life or even an IRS audit, it is freedom to know that they don't own you.

Homer depicted humanity as playthings of the gods. For Homer, the only hope for us is to leave home, to venture forth, to stand up on our own two feet, heroically to strike out, to make a name for ourselves, to outwit our grim fate through our actions. Jesus depicts us as those who have a home, a Father who waits, and whose lives are caught up in a larger story than that of our own devising. We call it grace.

Please note: Unlike Homer's *Odyssey*, Jesus' story doesn't have an ending. We are not told if the younger brother ever grew up or if the older brother ever came in and joined the party. We doubt that they "lived happily ever after." (I told you this was a true story.) Jesus doesn't end the story because this is the story which you finish yourself. I'm betting that the one on whom the Father is waiting, the one whom he is begging to come in, and party, is YOU. This story says that you journey not alone. There is One who names you, claims you, has plans for you, waits or prods, invites or blesses you. This One, sooner or later, will have you.

"O LORD, you have searched me, and you know me. You know when I sit and when I rise; . . . You discern my going out and my lying down, . . . You hem me in behind and before; you have laid your hand upon me. . . .Where can I go from your Spirit? Where can I flee from your presence?" (Psa. 139:17, AP)

For Further Reflection

1. How did you get to where you are today in your relationship with God?

2. In what ways have you sensed that you were owned, claimed by God?

3. Think about the difference between describing our lives as our creations and construing our lives as part of God's larger story.

4. Who serves as a faith mentor to you? Have you encouraged another person in the community of faith? If so, how did you encourage the person?

2

The Pain of
Salvation

Crime and Punishment

*I tell you, unless a grain of wheat falls into the earth
and dies, it remains just a single grain; but if it dies, it
bears much fruit.*

—John 12:24

Fyodor Dostoyevsky was haunted by God. He spent his
whole life running away from, and wrestling with, God. It
was only toward the end of his life that he at last felt that
he had passed through what he called "the hell-fire of doubt."

"Accept suffering and be redeemed by it," Dostoyevsky said
to a world much like our own, a world in which suffering was
rendered meaningless, in which the whole world sought to abol-
ish suffering and find happiness by puffing up the ego to the
level of deity.

Surely Dostoyevsky would agree with contemporary novelist
Bernard Malamud who, when asked whether suffering was
essential for good writing, said of suffering, "I'm against it but
when it occurs why waste the experience?"

Before it is a great spiritual novel, Dostoyevsky's *Crime and
Punishment* is a great detective story, a murder mystery which
nearly anyone could read with relish. It is also a great love story.
But, as the title says, it is about crime, a terrible crime, and pun-

ishment, a terrible punishment which, by the end of the novel, is also a source of grand, painful redemption.

After a violent crime, the life of a self-confident young murderer begins slowly to unravel. A Columbo-like detective, Lieutenant Powder, at first appearing bumbling and inept, begins to take apart the psyche of the young criminal until at last he breaks and confesses. It is a story repeated often since Dostoyevsky told it, but never again told so well.

I first met Raskolnikov in high school, which is as good a time as any. In *Crime and Punishment* he is introduced to us as the prototype of the young, intelligent, self-confident, though misanthropic and troubled modern youth. Like many young people in any age, Raskolnikov feels as if he is the first person in the history of the world to stand upon his own two feet, to think as he thinks, and to feel as he feels. Other people are idiots. He is a genius, therefore he is free from the old morality. He must make up the rules as he goes.

Raskolnikov is thus the first modern man. For what is modernity if not the attempt to stand alone, to decide for ourselves, to choose, to fabricate our own lives? Modernity is the story that we are free to choose our own stories, to craft our own identity. In fact, in the modern world, choice was for the first time said to be the very essence of humanity. I choose, therefore I am. No longer need one be determined by family, parents, race, nation, neighborhood, church. I can choose. Ironically, the story that I ought to choose my life for myself is also a story that I did not choose, a dogma, though a dogma which attempts to silence all other dogma.

To demonstrate his super-human, modern freedom of choice, Raskolnikov plans the perfect crime. He will make manifest his super-human courage and creativity by murdering one of the world's lesser creatures. Raskolnikov murders an old woman, a money-lender and, by happenstance, her sister, Elizabeth, who just happens to be there when the murder occurs. Raskolnikov has judged the old lady to be an utterly useless member of society, a rich, miserly old fool. The murder of the old woman is described by Raskolnikov as a means of proving "to himself that he was a man and not a louse," a kind of heroic lashing out. Yet his murder of the sister is random, without justification or any meaning.

His horrendous crime is without passion or much motive. He bashes in her head in a cool, detached manner, for the murder is (as he sees it) more an experiment in freedom than a crime, a demonstration of Raskolnikov's analytical mind, a mind which prides itself for its inability to love or to feel.

The psychotherapist, Erich Fromm, declared that intellectuals killed God in the eighteenth century so that they might destroy humanity in the nineteenth century. Dostoyevsky wrote against this background, the background of the birth of the modern world. It was a world this somber, perhaps mad Russian was loathe to celebrate declaring, "Without God, everything is permitted." *Crime and Punishment* may be Dostoyevsky's demonstration of the depths to which our newfound "freedom" would descend before we were done being free. He has Dmitri Karamazov say, in *The Brothers Karamazov,* that there is a war going on in the world in which "God and the Devil strive for mastery, and the battleground is the heart of men."

But Dostoyevsky's concerns are more than merely moral. He makes little judgment upon the crime. "Good" or "bad" are not his main interest. Most contemporary critics think of *Crime and Punishment* as the first great psychological novel of the modern era. Modern people tend to describe everything in terms of psychology.

I think of *Crime and Punishment* more as a great spiritual novel, an account of someone's path back to God, a path not taken by desire or decision but rather through the relentless, somber persistence of God. Perhaps more accurately we ought to describe this novel as God's path back toward a troubled soul. And the path is not pleasing.

The first step on the way to Raskolnikov's painful redemption comes through the love of Sonia, a Russian woman of the streets, a woman who has become a prostitute in order to help her stepmother who is dying of tuberculosis. She is described as a person who, for Raskolnikov, has "insatiable compassion." In admiration of her passion and compassion, Raskolnikov falls to the ground and kisses her foot, as if overwhelmed by her vibrant, passionate humanity. Yet he later dismisses Sonia as a "religious fanatic." Her persistent, patient, pure love will figure heavily in his final redemption.

The story which Dostoyevsky tells in *Crime and Punishment* is rich, too rich to summarize here. Most of the story goes on in Raskolnikov's brain as he begins to unravel, to be tormented by the questions of the police, the thought of his crime, the swirling self-doubt and fear. In great torment, Raskolnikov submits to Sonia, finally willing to take her way of public confession in an attempt to rid himself of his great burden. Sonia has told him that the only way to find peace is publically to acknowledge his great crime, to submit to God, to repent.

Toward the end of the novel, frayed and disordered, he comes to her saying, "I have come to bear the cross, Sonia. It was you advised me to go and make a public confession."

Sonia, woman of the streets, becomes transformed into virginal purity and light. Sonia becomes as Jesus' mother, Mary, accompanying Raskolnikov down that narrow, difficult, humiliating but finally liberating path toward confession. Sonia produces two little crosses, hanging one made of cypress (symbolizing mourning and death) around his neck. "This is a symbolic way of showing that I am taking a cross upon myself, hah! hah! As if this were my first day of suffering!" says Raskolnikov.

Earlier, when the old landlady had attempted to give him a little cross, he had flung it back in her face. But that was a long time ago. "Is the game really up?" he asks himself as he makes his way out into the street to make his confession. He realizes now that he is not a great, courageous rebel, a cunning criminal. Compared to the serene and pious Sonia, he is a miserable little coward who can neither sin boldly nor confess nobly.

The market-place was now full of people. This fact displeased Raskolnikov greatly; nevertheless he went to that part of it where the crowd was thickest. He would have bought solitude at any price, but he felt that he could not enjoy it for a single moment. Having got to the center of the place, the young man suddenly recalled Sonia's words: "Go to some public place, bow to the crowd, kiss the earth you have soiled by your sin, and say in a loud voice, in the presence of everyone: 'I am a murderer.'" At the recollection of this he trembled in every limb. The anguish of the last few days had hardened his heart to such an extent, that he felt satisfied to find himself still open to feelings of another kind, and gave himself entirely up to this one. Sincere sorrow overpowered him, his eyes filled with tears. He knelt in the very middle of the place, bowed earthwards, and joyfully kissed the miry ground. After having risen, he knelt down once more.

"There's a fellow who has got a tile loose!" observed a lad standing by.

This observation was received with shouts of laughter.

"He is a pilgrim bound for Jerusalem, boys; he is taking leave of his children and his native land; he is wishing everybody good-bye, even St. Petersburg and the ground of the capital," added a respectable man, slightly the worse for drink.

"He is very young," said a third. . . .

On seeing himself the object of general attention, Raskolnikov lost his self-possession somewhat, and the words: "I have killed," which he had on the tip of his tongue, died away. . . . he had perceived Sonia at a short distance from him. The girl had done her best to escape his observation, . . . She was, therefore, accompanying him while he was ascending his

Calvary! From that moment Raskolnikov acquired the certainty that Sonia was his for ever, would follow him anywhere, even if destiny were to lead him to the end of the world. He entered the courtyard with a tolerably firm footstep.

Raskolnikov staggers into the police station, there to encounter his great nemesis, Lieutenant Powder, who exasperatingly engages him in all sorts of trivialities and small talk. He chatters on in seemingly marked obliviousness to Raskolnikov's suffering. Finally comes the confession.

Still, the teller of this tale says that, through the trial and immediate aftermath, Raskolnikov admitted to one and only one crime—"a silly error." He has confessed, but he has not repented. His old self still struts, even in prison. The worst thing about his prison sentence was his terribly wounded pride. Sonia came to visit him at his prison in the first days, but he behaved contemptibly toward her. He considers himself superior to the other convicts at the prison. When Sonia comes to visit, all the other convicts treat her with great honor and respect, which Raskolnikov resents.

Then Raskolnikov falls seriously ill. During his illness, he has a dream in which the whole world is seized by a terrible plague. (Dostoyevsky is big on these strange dreams.) All die of the disease "except a few elect." These elect were afflicted with a strange sense that all of their thoughts and judgments were wise and absolutely correct. "They were incapable of understanding one another, because each believed himself the sole possessor of truth,. . . They could not agree upon any point, didn't know what to consider evil, what good, and they fell upon one another in anger and killed, they formed great armies, but, once in motion, they tore each other to pieces."

In the world of the dream, all trade was abandoned, famine set in, and many perished—except for a new elect, pure and good, who were left to purify and to populate the earth, though none recognized them or "knew their voices or heard their words." What on earth did this dream mean? Raskolnikov asked himself. I wonder if it is not a glimpse of the world as we have made it—modern chaos and violent confusion. Yet amid all of the troubles, amid the Promethean arrogance of modernity and its wreckage, there are the pure—of whom Sonia is the most noble representative.

She represents the only way out, the only way forward. This once despised woman shows Raskolnikov the way toward God through suffering, self-loss, and repentance. Shortly after his dream, she is there to meet him. Now he sleeps with a New Testament under his pillow, the same book from which Sonia once read to him of the raising of Lazarus. Raskolnikov becomes a new Lazarus, one who having died is raised back to life. He had thought that, once he went to jail, Sonia would be forever pestering him about religion but, "to his astonishment, she never spoke of religion, nor even mentioned the Scriptures." Through her prayers and patient, loyal waiting on him, she has led Raskolnikov back to God. Sonia has simply waited for life to take its toll upon Raskolnikov, waiting in the wings until, stripped of all his pretention and pride, he is ready to see Light.

He goes to his seven years of exile and imprisonment thinking that they would be like only seven days. Sonia will wait for him. He has now learned, says Dostoyevsky, "that new life is not given for nothing; that it has to be paid dearly for, and only acquired by much patience and suffering, and great future efforts."

New life, forgiveness, redemption and a fresh start are offered to all, but not without cost, not without the ordeal of patience and suffering. This was Dostoyevsky's vision. As Dostoyevsky began work on *The Brothers Karamazov*, his most complex and wonderful novel, his first notation in his writer's notebook was, "Find out whether it's possible to lie between the rails with a train passing over you at full speed."

That bit of information would not only play a role in that novel, but it might also be used to characterize all of Dostoyevsky's great books, especially *Crime and Punishment:* the great, dark engine of God terrifyingly passes over the souls of characters like Raskolnikov at full speed.

It is not a particularly appealing way to reach enlightenment or to be saved, but it is at least an orthodox Christian way:

> Let the same mind be in you that was in Christ Jesus, who, though he was in the form of God, did not regard equality with God as something to be exploited, but emptied himself, taking the form of a slave, being born in human likeness. And being found in human form, he humbled himself and became obedient to the point of death—even death on a cross.
>
> —Phillippians 2:5-8

This is the way Paul took, or rather the way which Christ took toward Paul as described in Acts 9:1-9. Saul was struck down, blinded, made helpless, had to be led by the hand, like a little child (Acts 9:7-9).

When I first came to work as chaplain at the university, a young man came to me for counseling. He had been suffering from depression since graduation. Having lost all self-confidence, he had done little since graduation, had been unable to go out and apply for a job, or to go out with friends.

I sat across from this healthy looking, muscular young man at the alleged prime of his life as he spoke incongruously of how "weak," he felt, how "vulnerable," he felt before the challenges of life.

"It's funny," he said. "I had more self-assurance when I was a high school senior than I do now that I'm a college graduate."

I blurted out, "I can explain that to you. At eighteen, high school hero, block letter sweater, world at your feet, you were stupid! Now, having taken a few tough courses, having failed a couple of times, having learned some of your limits, you have grown wise. Most men in this culture don't learn what you know until after their first heart attack at forty. Rejoice! You're a fast learner!"

I remind you that Jesus said that we can't get into the Kingdom of God unless we "turn and become as a little child." That downward turning can be painful, very painful in our society which worships success and achievement and power.

Years ago, Sigmund Freud complained in *The Economic Problem of Masochism* that novels like *Crime and Punishment* pushed a morbid sense of self-negation which, according to Freud, was unhealthy: ". . . masochism creates a temptation to perform 'sinful' actions, which must then be expiated by the reproaches of the sadistic conscience (as exemplified in so many Russian character types)."

Poor Freud. He could imagine no other way toward enlightenment than that way which becomes ever more absorbed by the self. Dostoyevsky surely knew that he was going against everything we believe in when, in dedicating his epic, *The Brothers Karamazov,* he quoted Jesus: "Verily, verily, I say unto you, Except a corn of wheat fall into the ground and die, it abideth alone: but if it die, it bringeth forth much fruit" (John 12:24, KJV).

Alas, too often contemporary, American evangelical Christianity has presented Christ as the means whereby we get everything we want and more, a surefire way to make basically well-to-do people even better off, three easy steps toward spiritual bliss.

Dostoyevsky spoke of another way, a more orthodox, more biblical way, the narrow way of self-denial, abnegation, and loss. It is the way which speaks of the cross, before it dares to speak of a crown, a way in which we go forward by first falling back and we turn and become as helpless and needy as a little child.

As pastor, I have often been moved by how people come forward for the Eucharist. They come to the Lord's Supper with empty hands outstretched, open, ready, and receptive. What an unusual posture this is for most contemporary Americans. We live in a society where we are constantly urged to "get hold of ourselves," to "find ourselves," to tightly grasp things in our hands and to hold on tight. Then comes the invitation to the Lord's Table. Then begins the training in letting go, in releasing our tight grip upon ourselves and all those false securities to which we so tightly cling. Then we come forward with empty hands, outstretched, open, hungry, needy, ready to receive a gift. Thus we are redeemed.

For Further Reflection

1. In what ways have you known, in your own life, the way of painful repentance, a self-emptying turning away from self and toward God?

2. Have you experienced a path to God as more painful than pleasant? How has your community experienced pathways to God? What is the difference between self-satisfaction and joy— or is there no distinction?

3. How is Christ asking you to "turn and become as a little child"?

3

To See the God We Had Not Asked to See

The Book of Job

I had heard of you by the hearing of the ear,
but now my eye sees you.

—Job 42:5

When I first read the Book of Job, back in college, I thought it was a book about innocent suffering. Job sounded to us sophomores like some protoexistentialist, when existentialism was all the rage. I've never been quite happy with that characterization. Even in my sophomoric mind, I knew that Job was too full, too rich to be characterized as a mere protest against the injustice of God, particularly in its ending. Dr. Carol Newsom, speaking at the 1995 Stetson Pastors School, suggested that the Book of Job is about more than simply getting across a message that God is just or that God is unjust. This book, says Newsom, is about nothing less than "the re-creation of our moral world."

In a way, every book is about that, for every book seeks to create a "world." Each of us lives in a "world" constructed of all the images, stories, myths, and insights which tell us what the world is and where it is heading. One of the ways our "world" is constructed is by the way we talk.

Newsom says that the Book of Job consists of a contest between rival ways of talking and the different moral imaginations thereby created. Each "voice" of Job expresses a different moral world.

Consider the overall structure of Job. Frankly, organization is one of the maddening things about reading Job. Things seem to repeat themselves; arguments stop and start and are later reiterated. The beginning is rather outrageous and the ending has exasperated readers for centuries.

Job begins with a "Once-upon-a-time" introduction, in a traditional narrative fashion. It begins to sound like a fairy tale. The very manner of speaking tells us that we are in a traditional world with a beginning, middle, and end. God is in his heaven and all is right in the world, at least in the beginning.

"There was once a man in the land of Uz whose name was Job. That man was blameless and upright, one who feared God and turned away from evil" (Job 1:1).

Then, there is trouble. "Let's see how faithful this Job is," says Satan. "Take away all of his blessings, and he will curse you to your face" (Job 1:11, AP).

Through a couple of tests, Job remains faithful. Then he sits in silence for seven days, and finally blurts out a harrowing curse of the day of his birth. Prose gives way to poetry, as if prose cannot carry the weight of the emotion to be expressed:

"Let the day perish in which I was born. . . . Let that day be darkness!" (3:3,4)

Now begins a long, rather tedious battle that takes all of twenty-five chapters while Job and his friends argue with one another about what is going on in the world. The friends are defenders of traditional morality, speaking a conventional, fixed, cause-and-effect world view. With "friends" like these, Job doesn't need enemies!

Finally Job ends the dialogue with a great oath, and a vehement protest of his innocence. After a fourth and annoyingly redundant argument by Elihu, finally God appears.

"Where were you when I laid the foundation of the earth?

Tell me, if you have understanding. Who determined its measurements—surely you know!" (38:4, AP)

But God says nothing about Job's guilt. Instead, God poses a long series of rhetorical questions, none of which seem to respond to the matters at hand.

When Job finally gets his opportunity to answer God's ravings, it is with brief words of humility. The friends are rebuked. Job's fortunes are restored. End of story.

As a plot, it's not much. But the plot of Job may not be the point. Perhaps, as Newsom suggests, it's the language, the way of speaking, which is the power of Job. In each way of speaking, there are different claims about the "real world." There are differences in what each of Job's friends say, but more important are the differences in how they say what they say. They structure their arguments differently and imbedded in these different ways of talking are different moral imaginations.

In the closing speeches from the whirlwind, God talks in very weird ways about various types of weird animals. The images and metaphors offered by God create a different moral world from that of Job and his friends. They lead us into unfamiliar territory where we are made to reconsider our definitions of "the real world."

The plot of the Book of Job proceeds by asking the reader to consider various ways of conceiving the moral life, moving from the naive to the more sophisticated. Finally we are led to reject the moral world which is rendered by the speeches of the friends in favor of Job's way of conceiving the moral world, which is finally superseded by God's way of talking about the world.

When it all ends, and the dust settles after the voice from the whirlwind, the writer takes up again that naive prose tale which has begun the Book of Job.

"I know that you can do all things, and that no purpose of yours can be thwarted" (42:1).

As a college student, I well remember how outraged I was by this pedestrian, "and they lived happily ever after" sort of ending. It seemed a cop-out. Here Job had raised such large, penetrating, existential questions, only to cave in at the end and submit to the traditionalist view that God is good and always rewards good people with good things.

Besides this, the final insertion of Elihu's speech in chapters 32-37 (with each chapter beginning, "Elihu continued and said. . . ." as if to say "Elihu went on and on and on and. . . .") also seems out of place, seems to drag us back to an earlier naive way which has been previously rejected. One wonders if Job was compiled poorly, if the writer, or writers had poor powers of organization with all this jumping back and forth.

Carol Newsom says that the way the Book of Job is put together retains a richness of voices. With so many voices in conflict, with this returning to earlier arguments, there is no final and decisive word, no final, official, utterly decisive way of conceiving of the moral life. Time and again in Job we think that the final decisive word has been spoken only to have the rug pulled out from under us by another voice speaking forth another "world." We think we are at last done with one argument and moved on to another only to have that argument return and reassert itself. Job is "multivocal" rather than "univocal." Voices keep intruding, keep clashing with other voices. The reader is surely meant to listen in on the argument at times, hearing his or her own voice, at times being challenged by the counter-voices.

The first voice in Job is a prose tale in Chapters 1 and 2. Its use of language reflects a distinctive moral imagination. It begins in a simple style. "A man there was in the land of Uz, and Job was his name." A few opening verses tell us a great deal about Job. Job is a man of character and wealth. He is described in simple, direct language. The narrator is offering to tell us the story that we already know, not only because the story of Job was known throughout the Near East at this time, but also because each of us knows this story from the tales of childhood. It is a story about good things happening to good people, a tale of righteousness rewarded.

We have entered a world of shared traditional moral values and myths, law and order, "family values," and all that. We are dealing with the inherited stories. The community is harmoniously regathering around its common myths. The words are simple; the syntax undemanding. Meaning is unproblematic. Everything is tidy. All fits in a clear, easy-to-follow, coherent picture. The narrator does not say there is a cause-effect relationship in morality. Doesn't have to.

In this world, things fit.

The story in these early chapters is told in brief, well-defined scenes with much repetition, which gives an air of predictability. It is a conventional moral world, where judgments can be asserted with confidence.

In the beginning, the narrator makes the judgments. He tells us what is what. The narrative asserts and illustrates. We readers are invited to confirm, through these illustrations, what the narrator says about the judgments.

In all things, Job never sinned. One cannot lose one's way in this secure moral world where things are stated and confirmed by both the narrator and God. Even when he faces terrible misfortune, Job is able to assert, "Naked I came from the womb, and naked I shall return to the dust" (1:21, AP), words trustworthy, proverbial, traditional, and true, as if they have quotes around them. Conventional wisdom.

In a chaotic moral time like ours, people return to proverbial, definitive truths. In a time of chaos, we return to stories that confirm and conform to traditional values. There is a great deal of talk, here in the beginning of Job, about traditional values, family, retribution, and reward. Reliable moral judgments are based on such a secure, stable moral world, it would seem. Goodness is not corrupted by wealth and social rank.

Carol Newsom asks, "What price does one pay to inhabit this moral world and adopt its moral imagination?" Unity, clarity, and order are affirmed here. But those qualities also describe the limits of such a world rendered by such a language, says Newsom. "The very qualities which make this moral world round, smooth, and shiny as a pearl, also are its great disadvantages." Is Job's initial response to his tragedy pious submission—I came into this world naked, having nothing, I will leave with nothing—or blind devastation? You make the call.

All might be well in this world if there were no intrusion, no conflict, no misfortune. Conflict intrudes into the story with the appearance of Satan, the accuser. Satan is here some heavenly being charged with spying on the world. The accusing angel and God share a common concern—uncovering true piety. The accusing angel says, "Of course Job is pious; you make it worth his while. But what if you withdrew your rewards?" (1:6-11, AP)

When Job at last speaks his stunning, howling words, he does so with heroism, with poetry and drama. His words, "That day, let that day be darkness," are a dramatic reversal of the words with which we began our story with God in Genesis: "That day, let there be light." See? The world is being deconstructed. This is sharp contrast to the way Job spoke earlier. Now, language is being pushed to its limit. Prose is cracking open into poetry. Someone has said that poetry is violence done to prose. The language of tradition is now being challenged. Job has not technically cursed God, but he is coming quite close. Ambiguity is being introduced. By changing the nature of language, and Job's relationship to language, the narrator has decisively opened up our discourse and thereby our world.

Job's speech lets loose a flood of talk. Words cannot now be held back. Everything is now off the table for open discussion. Thus William Safire once called Job "The First Dissident." Job the silent sufferer becomes Job the verbose complainer. Now, because of Job's eloquent complaint, a world which was previously settled, fixed, and absolute, has to be defended and argued explicitly by Job's friends. The center will now not hold without some defense, and defenders appear in the speeches of the "friends."

In the speeches of the friends, Newsom notes that the authoritative voice of the narrator vanishes. Now there is only adversarial speech, a free-for-all verbal battle and moralistic one-upmanship.

This manner of speaking allows us readers to listen, to compare for ourselves what is going on, to take sides, to rethink our values and opinions. We are now entering into radically different images of what the world may be like, morally speaking.

Implicit in this is an affirmation that this kind of speech against speech is the way that we may eventually come toward what is true. This speech believes that the way to truth is through argument, conflict, a free market of moral ideas.

For all of this interaction between the friends, Job remains committed to the stance that somewhere there is absolute, unassailable truth. Absolute truth can be found, so Job will listen in the hope that he will eventually be able again to affirm that absolute truth.

The clash of different speeches, which is rather invigorating in the first round of speeches, begins to be tiresome by the second round and excruciatingly tedious by the third. Why is the third cycle of speeches here at all? It all sounds so confused and conflicted. Newsom says that perhaps this third, confused and disordered cycle is meant to be a symbol of the failure of speech and dialogue to resolve these issues.

If you have ever been part of a community which tried to find truth only by argument, voice attacking voice, truth found on the basis of whoever is left standing by the end of the debate, you know how tiresome all this can be where virtues are merely reiterated, over and over with no real speaking or listening.

Newsom offers a wonderful thesis about that strange interlude in Chapter 28: "Surely there is a mine for silver, and a place for gold to be refined. Iron is taken out of the earth, and copper is smelted from ore. Miners put an end to darkness, and search out to the farthest bound the ore in gloom and deep darkness" (28:1-3).

The chapter which follows these speeches, Chapter 28, appears to be a nonsequitur. It is cool and unemotional, somewhat of a relief after all this redundant shouting by the friends. Still it's strange. For eleven verses Chapter 28 describes the marvelous human capacity for mining precious things from the earth. Finally it tells us what this mining expedition was all about. Where will Wisdom be found (28:12)? How can the human being mine Wisdom? It is not found in the land of the living.

Evidently, this interlude is a comment on the futility of the arguments by the friends. Job and his friends will never be able to dig their way to Wisdom with the tools of their assertive speech.

Only God has found wisdom. Wisdom is only with the Lord. Thus the narrator intrudes to invite the reader to give up the incoherent, cacophony of disputation and return home to trusted, traditional wisdom. All you need to know is what you knew at the beginning, which you should never have left.

At this point, if the end of this story were Job recanting and giving up his arguments against God, then this would be an artful William Bennett-like defense of traditional, proverbial wisdom and little more. However, the story is not yet done.

Elihu returns as a catalyst to Job's speech. After Chapter 28, we hear Job's words. Though Job sounds broken, submissive, he still holds out hope that the order of the universe still holds. Job still seeks a definitive answer, a definitive encounter with God.

At last comes the speech of the Lord. What Job wants is a day in which he would question God and God would give definitive answers. But the dialogue never quite takes place. Once again, the way language is used changes. We enter into a world of a very different moral imagination.

The God whom Job wants to question becomes the questioner. Moveover, God never addresses the issues which Job so eloquently raised. Ultimately, the result of God's speech is to end Job's speech. "I have put my hand over my mouth. I have spoken once, I will not speak twice" (40:4-5, AP).

When Job replies again at the beginning of chapter 42, he begins with his words, but ends up by quoting God's words. Job devalues his own speech. He recites God's words.

"Therefore I have uttered what I did not understand, things too wonderful for me, which I did not know. . . . I had heard of you by the hearing of the ear, but now my eye sees you" (42:3, 5).

No more is Job subverting the words of God, as he did in the beginning, when he cursed the day of his birth in order to reverse God's work in creation. Now, Job speaks words of authority, quotes from God.

God speaks simply with the voice of authority, ending all dialogue, asserting, stopping all other speech. God's speech ought to be done with megaphone in hand, shouting, overpowering. However, there is more to divine speech than just the display of authoritarian power. God does put an end to Job's questions. However, in God's speech is also a glimpse of a remarkable vision of the cosmos. God invites Job to look at the vision, as if for the first time.

Look at the world, just for a moment, as God looks at the creation. There are wonders here beyond human comprehending. Elusive. God brags about the works of creation, the mysteries, the wonders. The Rabbis long ago noted that, when God boasts of his handiwork, of all the animals God offers as evidence of divine creative genius, none of them is of any earthly use to humanity! What can you do with a wild ass or an ostrich? Moreover, when bragging about wonderful animals, God fails ever to mention pride at the creation of humanity! It's a big creation out there; humanity is only a small part of its wonder.

The divine speech has teased the imagination. The speech from the whirlwind has thwarted Job's expectations, forced open conventional constraints on perception. This is not merely the voice of authority, requiring submission. This is the voice of a very wide view of the world which seeks not just submission but new seeing.

Walter Brueggemann has said that he sees Job "as a recognition of a world that is falling apart and in which the pain of such displacement is acute." Yet the pain eventually leads to "an incredible leap beyond Israel's known world."

Is not this what Job says at the end? "I had heard of you by the hearing of the ear, but *now my eye sees you*" (42:5, italics mine). Previously, Job had only heard tell of a God who sets the world in motion, who creates out of chaos; now Job sees. Any moral imagination allows for only a limited range of vision in a conflicted moral situation. When one comes across contradictions which refuse to fit in the span of our moral horizon, our world falls apart. Job inhabited a rather myopic world of retributive and distributive justice, where people get what they deserve, where there is a just God to see that all get what they deserve. But then come the contradictions. Job suffers; is he guilty? Is God fair?

All of this cannot be held together within the conventional vista. The friends try, but fail. All they can offer is the sacrifice of Job's innocence. "Surely you must have done something to deserve this," they say in various ways.

On the other hand, to make the contradictions fit, Job was willing to sacrifice God's fairness. "Surely God is not all he has been made up to be," Job says in various ways.

A woman in my church who said to me, standing in a hospital corridor, "If my daughter dies, I will never play the piano in church again." The daughter died; the mother kept her word. When our world of cause-effect morality crumbles, then we are devastated. Our world has been dismantled. Will anything take its place?

Job is invited out toward a new world, a world not based upon simple, distributive, retributive justice. What does Job decide? We really don't know. Carol Newsom points out that Job's words are linguistically ambiguous. The Hebrew can be taken at least a couple of ways. What does he really say here at the end in 42:6? Does he say, "I take back what I said and I repent in dust and ashes?" Or does he say, "Therefore I retract my words and repent of dust and ashes?" That is, does he say, as the New Revised Standard Version implies, "I repent of my alienation and grief from God?" Or does he say, "I repent and am now comforted concerning my previous bout with dust and ashes?" The Hebrew is confusing, difficult to translate.

So even at the end, there is an irresistible ambiguity. Even at the end. How different this is than the opening paragraph of Job. Thus the language teases the reader with multiple possibilities.

Yet perhaps even more surprisingly, just as we are getting comfortable with this complex, ambiguous, rich and new way of seeing the world—"Job, the world is vast and incomprehensible. I created it, but I can't explain it to all to you"—the story takes one last surprising turn. The language of the book changes yet once again and we are back in the world of the prose tale.

"And the LORD restored the fortunes of Job when he had prayed for his friends; and the LORD gave Job twice as much as he had before" (Job 42:10). Ironically, where once this language functioned, at the beginning of Job, as a clear didactic statement of tidiness, now, the very first verses of the prose conclusion seem to have God endorsing Job's earlier speech!

I know of no way to smooth out the contradictions. Must we say this is a result of bad editing and historical jumbling? Here God declares Job's indictments correct! I now see, with the aid of Carol Newsom, this ending as sly acknowledgment that there is something to be said for Job's indictment of God. Rebuked as Job may be, still, there is something to be said for his charges against God. Even after God has had his day in court, questions still remain after the voice from the whirlwind.

Job has discredited the friends and God has rebuked the friends, but still what do the friends say? At the heart of what they say is that there is justice and fairness in God's world. God does not punish good people without restoration of their fortunes. As a contemporary reader I delight that this traditionalist line of reasoning is eloquently refuted, but then I am forced to admit that this is just what happens by the end of the book! Job is restored. His family continues. God has come to Job and finally spoken to him. God may say that the friends are wrong, but the outcome of the story says that the friends are right.

The whole structure of the latter part of the book piles ambiguity on ambiguity and contradiction on contradiction. I can't pin the meaning down. Modern man that I am, I want my truth in simple, reduced, straightforward facts. Thus, my modern moral horizon tends to be myopic. The Book of Job teases me toward a wider view. It enables me to see a great God of whom I had only previously heard.

I can't have the last word about the Book of Job. Nobody can. What does this teasing and even frustrating ending, with the obscurity of the final word, suggest about the book as a whole?

It asks us to think about meaning differently. Here, at the end, we are not asked to choose which meaning is ultimately authoritative. Meaning does not come through critical discernment. It comes aesthetically, by a new way of seeing. At the end, I don't get answers. I get a deepened relationship with God. God doesn't come with easy answers; God comes offering presence.

Each voice has said something true, something which does make sense. And yet nothing is finally closed and fixed and finished. In the end, with God, it's relationship rather than reasons that keeps us going in the tragic, chaotic, inexplicable times of our lives.

Like Job, I've got to learn to live in a world full of many conflicting moral voices, none of which decisively triumphs over another. Nothing can be homogenized into a single authoritative voice. The phrase "simple truth" tends to be oxymoronic. So as we grapple with similarly complex questions, we must beware of homogenization and smoothing. Conflict remains, after much, very much, has been said.

God comes to us not with answers but with God's self, with a way of seeing rather than a way of simple understanding. We need all of these voices, all of these partial ways of seeing. All of the voices have some truth in them and need to be heard. No one alone can speak the last word, the word of God.

A literary critic, Jack Miles, attempted to read the Bible as if he were reading a play or a novel, using the techniques of contemporary literary criticism. What sort of character is being rendered in this book, the Bible? Namely, who is this God? Miles called his book, *God: A Biography*.

Miles notes that, as the Bible opens, God is very loquacious, always talking, so talkative that God even talks to himself in Genesis since, at this early date before Creation, there is no one else to join in the conversation. The creation of humanity is depicted as an attempt to create someone to listen to God's talk. God is forever talking, arguing, and interacting with God's human subjects. In the Book of Deuteronomy, God says that everything he has said is perfectly clear and understandable by any reasonably intelligent Israelite so everything God orders must be explicitly obeyed.

But after the Book of Job, says Miles, a change occurs. After Job, God ceases to do so much talking. God becomes rather remote, unapproachable, moody and mysterious.

That is (I would say to Miles) until the New Testament when God speaks saying, "This is my beloved Son, in whom I am well pleased" (Matt. 3:17, KJV).

Then, in Jesus, God comes to us, not with simple answers but as a Son, as Suffering Servant, as one who comes and stands beside us, suffering with us. In Jesus Christ we see as much of God as we ever hope to see. In Jesus, we get not simple answers. We get a vision. We see God.

Which we Christians have always believed to be better, even than answers.

For Further Reflection

1. In what ways have you mistakenly thought of yourself as the center of God's creation?

2. Do you "serve God for nothing," or is your service conditional on how well things go in your own life?

3. In what ways do your worship, prayer, Bible reading, and devotion enable you to get a wider vision of God?

4. How can you be open to God's presence? Are there times when God seems more present than other times? What have you noticed during these times?

4

Disciplined Goodness

Mr. Ives' Christmas

*And the Word became flesh and lived among us, and
we have seen his glory, . . . full of grace and truth.*
—John 1:14

"This is the season of joy, of peace, of goodwill and
love," thus explained the host of a televised Christmas
special, a gala event for the President and First Lady
featuring choirs, pop singers, and oodles of sugar-coated glitz.

How curious that someone would think Christmas is about any
such superficial trivialities, at least curious from a biblical point of
view. For it is almost as if the Gospels go out of their way to present the Incarnation not only as earthly, not only as mundane, but
carnal, even. After all, Incarnation means "enfleshment," meat.
"The Word became flesh and lived among us," says John.

Luke, always the consummate artist, depicted that enfleshing
of God so vividly that for most of us Christians, when we think
Nativity, we can do so only with the images which Luke gives.
Luke's narrative images are those of the stable and the cow pas-
ture, sheep, shepherds, and a peculiar pregnancy. Even a secular
world which rejects Luke's Christ can't get out of its mind the
images of Luke's Nativity.

Not much sentiment in the First Gospel either. Matthew's
exotic Magi are offset by the screams of Jewish mothers, Rachel

weeping for her slaughtered sons. Matthew's Nativity ends with the Holy Family fleeing as refugees to Egypt while Herod rages. It is politically violent, bloody, and disruptive. This is not the stuff of televison's "joy, peace, goodwill and love." The Bible is so realistic. If God Almighty should be born among us, among *us*, then the story must deal with our politics, violence, blood and dirt or it won't do us any good.

"Ives always looked forward to the holiday season." Thus begins Oscar Hijuelos' novel of a good man, Ives, and his Christmas memories. We are told that Ives loved to wander into New York's Saint Patrick's Cathedral around Christmas, to smell the candles, to savor the season, the kings, the angels, shepherds and baby Jesus. This is the stuff of a conventional Christmas story, sentiment mixed with Yuletide cheer. Yet we are warned that for Ives, Christmas is more than greeting card sentimentality. As for Christmas, "Nothing could please him more, nothing could leave him feeling a deeper despair."

Ives is a good man, at times almost too good to be true. He is exceptionally kind, caring, and compassionate. Hijuelos almost makes Ives too kind to be believable. He is an orphan, a devoted Catholic, courteous, unprejudiced and generous. His passionate love for Annie and their courtship provide a much-needed realistic, mundane counterweight to the almost saccharine depiction of Ives' character.

The novel begins at Christmas, remembering Christmases of the past. Annie and Ives decide to marry one Christmas. Later, one Christmas, tragedy rips Ives' world apart. Then, many Christmases after, Ives makes a bold, obedient move and starts toward redemption.

Church and Ives' vibrant practice of Catholicism figure prominently in the novel. Ives loves to go to church. He delights in teaching his young son, Robert, about Jesus and the rituals of the church. Robert responded well to his father's teaching. Indeed, it seemed as if the two had "two homes: their apartment and the church" (p. 73). Robert feels called into the Franciscan order. From his earliest childhood, Robert evidenced a deep religious sensitivity.

Although Ives has his moments of doubt (one time, when trapped with a young woman on a stuck elevator, he comes to question the depth of his own faith and "whether or not his devotion is mere mimicry of his father's religious mannerisms"), his practice of his Christianity pervades the novel, particularly his relationship with Robert.

Ives has a mystical experience (a clock aglow "with a kind of benevolent, supernatural light") in which he feels great reassurance despite his doubts. He tells no one of the experience, though that day, as he cheerfully helps an old lady with her bundle of packages on the subway, she commented, "My, you really do enjoy this holiday, don't you?"

Ives attempts to explain to her that his glow is due not just to the Christmas season but to "a vision of God's presence in the world" which Ives thought elicited from her the supposition that he "was not playing with a full deck of cards." Somehow he believed that, in the mystical vision, "he had been privy to the inner workings of God."

And then there was Christmas, 1967. Robert was a young man finishing school, preparing to enter the Franciscans. The Ives family had enjoyed its usual round of Christmas activity. After choir practice at their beloved Church of the Holy Ascension, Robert, aged seventeen, simply turned his head toward a fourteen-year-old hood and with a *pop-pop-pop* lay dead on the sidewalk.

Police quickly apprehended the young murderer who had bragged to his friends of having popped "a rich white boy." There was a funeral. Reporters made much of Robert's wholesome character ("A young man about to enter seminary") and the murderer's sordid police record. Daniel Gomez was Puerto Rican. His mother was on welfare. He was an eighth-grade dropout. Later, at the trial, Gomez had little reaction to his sentence—twenty years to life. His mother screamed. Ives and Annie began the long, dark, lonely journey which those in grief must walk.

"He went to church and prayed for guidance, begging God

to bring forgiveness into his heart." Kneeling before the cross and the crèche, he would wonder how Robert's death could happen, if this were God's will, and what, if anything, it all meant. An irony pervades the tragedy—Ives had always been close to Hispanic people. His best friends were Puerto Rican. He had studied Spanish and had quietly urged his company to hire and promote Hispanics.

Some of Ives' friends urge him to seek vengeance. One even presents him with a pistol. Ives doesn't want vengeance. But he does long for some way to take away the pain, the questions, the horrible ache within his soul, the ache which takes its toll on his health, his marriage, and his faith.

At the priest's urging, Ives consents to meet with the Gomez family. While Gomez's grandmother apologizes and begs Ives to forgive them, the boy's mother scorns the visit and insists on her son's innocence. She already has two sons in jail and now stands to lose a third "because he's dark and Puerto Rican."

The next day the newspaper printed a photography of Ives being embraced by Gomez' weeping grandmother. Over the picture was printed, "Forgiveness."

At this point we suspect the novel begins to be about forgiveness. Is it possible in this world among real people who have suffered terribly deep, terribly real wounds?

A group of Ives' friends urge him to secure the services of a Mafia hit-man. He looks into their "wolves' faces" and pleads, "Please, I beseech you. . . ."

One of them responds, "Beseech? Are we in the f---ing Bible?"

It's a good question. We have the feeling that, in this terrible, dark pain, in Ives' conflicted emotions, in this talk of retribution and forgiveness, we are moving toward a story which is becoming biblical. And we are. Ives continues to struggle with his grief. He sees a young priest at the altar in the Mass and thinks he sees Robert. He reads self-help books which urge grieving readers not to blame themselves for the tragedy, not to become alienated from the people they love, not to do this, to do that.

Still, Ives suffers, memories of *"that Christmas"* forever burned in his brain.

Not knowing how to feel as a Christian, or what to do, "Ives concluded that the only way to deal with suffering was to trust in God and cling to the path of righteousness: and this he did, despite his doubts, approaching the whole notion of his faith as a matter of will and discipline."

Will and discipline are not much in fashion in our age. In our minds, religion is mostly a matter of feelings—private, personal feelings—as we drift from one vaguely spiritual high to another, or else descend into the depths when we have no feeling left to muster. Faith reduced to personal feeling is no match for the really great tragedies of life. In his tragedy, Ives does what, in my pastoral experience, I have found that hurting Christians do. By sheer act of the will and force of discipline, he continues to believe, persists in the rites and practices of the church, keeps going to Mass, continues to celebrate the feasts of the church even though inside he feels anything but celebration.

Here is a strong devotional message of this novel, I believe. I don't always feel like a Christian, nor do I always think or act like a Christian. Fortunately, my faith is not a matter of my earnest efforts. Faith is a gift. But it is a gift offered through the offices of the church, the "means of grace," as we call the church's preaching and sacraments.

This, I believe, accounts for the quote from Clement Miles which Hijuelos prints on the first page of the novel: "It is difficult to be religious, impossible to be merry, at every moment of life, and festivals are, as sunlit peaks, testifying above dark valleys, to the eternal radiance."

In Ives' walk through the dark valley, it is church and its festivals, like Christmas, the Feast of the Incarnation, which keep him going, keep Ives determined to wrench some meaning and redemption out of his tragedy, keep him expecting that, through it all, God means some good to come from the bad. No one can be religious at "every moment of life." So God graciously gives us certain (in John Wesley's words) "ordinary means of grace" whereby our ordinary lives are kept tied to the holy and the righteous.

I think we have made a big mistake in implying that the spiritual life, our relationship to God, is mostly a matter of what feelings we manage to muster. My relationship to Christ is also a matter of keeping at it, of habits, of persisting in the disciplines of faith. Feelings are fine, as far as they go. But feelings are notoriously short-lived. Habits keep us close to God even when the feelings are not there.

You show me a marriage based only upon feelings, and I'll show you a short-lived affair. Most of us find that the love of marriage needs ritual, habit, and discipline to keep love in marriage. A marriage must develop and nourish opportunities to be together, to talk, to make love, to have fun, to hang out doing nothing, to work and serve together in activities outside the marriage if the relationship is to survive.

I believe this is a not too mundane analogy for our relationship to God. Many modern people say they feel far away from God. Yet is this sense of distance due to God's absence or our negligence? Is God dead or have we merely neglected the host of disciplined, habitual, acts of the will which keep us close to the God who (if the Incarnation is true) deems to be close to us? Disciplines, habits like reading the Bible, going to church, praying even when we don't feel like it, are the means whereby we are kept close to God, whereby we await a more vivid sense of God's nearness during the times when we, like Mr. Ives, must walk through some dark valley.

Mr. Ives' disciplines enable him to be prepared to move toward God. What is the "Christian" thing for him to do? He doesn't know. But he decides to write Gomez, the murderer of Robert, a letter. He sends Gomez some books, and a Bible. That begins a correspondence between Ives and Gomez. Ives sends a Christmas package of comic books and a radio. He urges Gomez to go back to school, to learn to read and write better. Annie doesn't understand these letters of Ives. She only desires that they could "move on" and put their son's death behind them. Ives is "moving on," but in a way which does not deny his faith that somehow God can work goodness even out of so terrible a tragedy as theirs.

One day he receives a letter. Daniel Gomez is out of jail. He has changed, he says, and has "found a little salvation." Ives doesn't know if Gomez is sincere. He doesn't know if he wants to see Gomez. He can't remember now if he wants to receive that which he had prayed to God so many years to grant, forgiveness for the man who murdered his son. Finally, on Christmas, he goes to see Gomez. They talk. Ives forgives and Gomez receives his forgiveness.

Some readers have found this final scene most unsatisfying. It is surprisingly undramatic. Gomez fumbles to express his gratitude for Ives' forgiveness. Ives feels a sense of relief afterward, but not too great a sense. It is all a bit anticlimactic after so long a struggle, after so deep a wound. But perhaps here is where Hijuelos is most realistic. Isn't this the way it often is in our lives? Christ commands us to forgive. When he commands us, he does not say that we will feel better afterwards, that all regrets are thereby made right, that the recipients of our forgiveness will go on to lead better lives. He simply commands us to forgive, to be perfect as God in heaven is perfect. We are to forgive, not as a strategy for achieving a more fulfilling life but simply because it is in the nature of God to forgive, because God's forgiveness is built into the foundation of the world, because, in forgiving we, like Ives, witness to the reign of a God who is forgiveness.

The novel ends with Ives in church, on Christmas, near the babe in the manger, his heart filled with a sense of the ultimate triumph of the goodness of God. That divine goodness is never completely evident in this world, in this life. Yet we do glimpse it, like Ives, in the mystical gifts of a God who wills to come among us, in our disciplined, willful acts of grace and courage such as the forgiveness of our enemies.

For Ives, Daniel Gomez is clearly the enemy, the one who thoughtlessly, cruelly, intruded upon his life. That Gomez was himself a kind of victim, one wounded by an unjust economic system, hurt by racism, poverty and ignorance, does not make it any easier for Ives. Our tragedies might be easier to bear if they were initiated by clearly evil, obviously bad people. In life, things are not so neat. It may be part of the essence of true tragedy that it is inherently messy, unresolved. Even after the mystical visions of God, after the courageous acts of forgiveness, there is still a surplus of pain, still something left over to be made right in some other time and place. Ives confesses, even at the end, to a certain bafflement at the meaning of it all.

Thus the novel ends, almost where it began, with Ives in church, in the Mass, his mind wandering to the crèche and the infant Jesus, to memories of wounds long ago, some healed, some still bleeding, and the Christ who left the manger for a cross. And perhaps there is a spiritual moral there for us, in this little parable of one man's relationship to the Christ. Like Ives, we don't always understand the bad that happens to us. Innocent suffering defies explanations. We don't always know what God is up to in our lives, or in the world. Things are not neat. There is regret, and things which could have worked out otherwise, and relationships that don't proceed as planned.

Understanding may not be the point. Maybe the point is simply to keep at it. Keep praying to God. Keep trying to be open to Christ's intrusions among us. Keep going to church, going through the motions, attending to matters of the Spirit out of habit, keep forgiving our enemies even when we don't feel like it or are uncertain of where it all leads. This, to me, is the great lesson of *Mr. Ives' Christmas.*

A public radio interviewer, talking with Oscar Hijuelos last Christmas, said, "Mr. Ives is so good, almost unbelievably good."

Hijuelos agreed, almost embarrassedly, and they spoke of something else.

I suppose that the sort of goodness by which a person musters the ability to forgive an enemy seems, to the world, a goodness too good to be true. Perhaps this is because the world, in its wisdom, is ignorant of the Incarnation. Believing that God came among us, in the flesh, dwelling where we live, walking

where we walk, tempted as we are tempted, Christians believe
that it is possible for us to come to God. Not by our own effort,
but rather through the incarnation of Christ, we are able to live
in the world as those who can forgive. In our weakness, the disciplines, rites, and sacraments of the church, God's incarnation,
enable us to be more than we could had not God in Christ come
among us.

For Further Reflection

1. List those spiritual disciplines which you follow "out of
habit" which keep you close to God.

2. How have you experienced your participation in the worship of the church as a means of grace, keeping you close to
God, even when you did not feel like it?

3. Have you ever forgiven an enemy? What would it take for
you to practice this sort of disciplined discipleship?

4. When have you been on the receiving end of forgiveness?
How does your community of faith forgive people?

5

To See
Ourselves As
God Sees Us

Revelation

I looked, and there was a great multitude that no one could count, from every nation, from all tribes and peoples and languages, standing before the throne and before the Lamb, robed in white, with palm branches in their hands. They cried out in a loud voice, saying, "Salvation belongs to our God who is seated on the throne, and to the Lamb!"

—Revelation 7:9-10

Psychotherapist Robert Coles says that he uses the stories of Flannery O'Connor in one of his classes at Harvard. I can't imagine what the bright, upwardly mobile, young students at Harvard make of O'Connor's unflinching honesty, her scathing humor. But perhaps I am selling Harvard short. O'Connor is determined to shock us into an awareness of the shakey foundation upon which our self-esteem is based, whereas we think we have done enough if we are appropriately "sensitive" to the needs or feelings of others. O'Connor is determined to hold the mirror of truth up to us until we are saved from our anxious attempts to save ourselves.

We live in a therapeutic age where most of us don't want to be saved, born again, or converted. We just want to feel better about ourselves. Everything is used as technique to enhance the

Holy Grail of our time—self-esteem. The only "sin" we know is the inability to think well of ourselves.

Our relentless care and affection for ourselves produces a rather thick coating of self-concern. Our well-polished self-images prove to be rather resilient to any real critique or honest self-evaluation. When asked why she made her characters so grotesque, such freakish representatives of the human race, Flannery O'Connor replied that only the freak, the truly outrageous and the grotesque could possibly hope to penetrate the crust of our self-deceit.

In *Revelation*, we join Mrs. Turpin in a doctor's waiting room. Mrs. Turpin sits there with her taciturn husband, Claud, described as a "lean stringy old fellow." Across from them sits (in Mrs. Turpin's description) a "white trash" woman with her sick child. Also a pleasant plain woman with her unattractive daughter whom Mrs. Turpin judges to be about eighteen or nineteen. The girl is reading a book.

Mrs. Turpin attempts to make conversation with the fellow waiting room inhabitants. In her mind she compares herself with them and comes off quite favorably. The "fat girl" bothers her with her silent, off-putting scowl, but Mrs. Turpin chatters on, despite the girl.

Sometimes, just before going to sleep at night, Mrs. Turpin would occupy herself with thoughts about "who she would have chosen to be if she couldn't have been herself," if Jesus had given her a choice of who she wanted to be. What if the only choices, in her mind and in her own words, were "white trash" or black? She was horrified at the thought. Mrs. Turpin has a very well developed social system in her mind, which, in her mind, God has ordained. She places each person she meets at various strata, with herself always at the top of the heap. On the bottom are the poor whites and poor blacks. She, with her manners, her pleasant disposition, and her positive outlook toward life, manages to sit serenely atop them all.

Still the ugly girl glares at her in a most disconcerting way; still Mrs. Turpin chatters condescendingly to the others as she carefully places each of them in her assigned human categories.

"One thang I don't want," says the "white-trash" woman with her child, "Hogs. Nasty stinking things, a-gruntin and a-rootin all over the place."

"Mrs. Turpin replies, "Our hogs are not dirty and they don't stink. . . .They're cleaner than some children I've seen. . . . We have a pig parlor." Even Mrs. Turpin's hogs are superior to the swine of others—certainly cleaner than the child of the woman sitting across from her.

Mrs. Turpin continues to chatter, as best as she can with the lowly creatures with whom she is confined in the waiting room. Hearing a song on the waiting room radio, she agrees with the saccharine lyrics, thinking to herself that she is a good person who always tries "to help anybody out that needed it. . . . whether they were white or black, trash or decent."

By this time she notes that the girl's "eyes were fixed like two drills" upon her. Noting that the girl is reading, Mrs. Turpin says, "You must be in college." She is determined to draw her out, determined to teach her polite manners. The girl says nothing. Her mother answers for her. Her name, it turns out, is Mary Grace. Mary Grace?

"It never hurt anyone to smile," says Mrs. Turpin, so the girl can hear her. "It just makes you feel better all over."

Then Mrs. Turpin muses, "If it's one thing I am, it's grateful. When I think of all I could have been besides myself . . . I just feel like shouting, 'Thank you, Jesus, for making everything the way it is!'"

The book hits Mrs. Turpin just over her left eye as she ends that statement. She sprawls on the floor as others scream, the girl is restrained and taken away but not before focusing on Mrs. Turpin and whispering in her ear, "Go back to hell where you came from, you old wart hog."

Now "Mrs. Turpin felt entirely hollow except for her heart which swung from side to side as if it were agitated by a great empty drum of flesh."

Mrs. Turpin, the once large, self-assured, confident woman is reduced to a hollow empty drum. She is descending to some hellish place where everything is strange, disrupted, cut loose. After being examined and patched up by the doctor, as she and Claud turn into the dirt road toward their house, she looks toward their home fully expecting to see "a burnt wound between two blackened chimneys," so terribly dislocated does she now feel.

Lying in bed that night, a damp washcloth over her eye, Mrs. Turpin repeats to herself tearfully, "I am not a wart hog from hell."

"But," writes O'Connor, "the denial had no force. . . . She had been singled out for the message, though there was trash in the room to whom it might justly have been applied. . . . The message had been given to Ruby Turpin, a respectable, hardworking, church-going woman." And the message was delivered by a girl named Mary Grace.

The next day Mrs. Turpin staggers down toward the hog pen, the "pig parlor" which once caused her such pride. "You look like you might have swallowed a mad dog," Claud says as he hands over the hose used for cleaning the hogs.

She stares at the hogs in their pen. She speaks words of fury, "How am I a hog and me both? How are I saved and from hell too?"

Martin Luther spoke of humanity under Christ as "at the same time justified and sinful." How can stripped, naked, pretentious, revealed liars like us (and now, after the girl's attack upon her, like Mrs. Turpin) be at the same time cherished and loved by God?

Mrs. Turpin has received a "revelation," delivered in the sneering words of the disturbed girl in the waiting room. For one stunning, terrible moment she has been made to gaze in the mirror of truth and to see her life as it is—a poorly constructed sham built over her put-downs of everything else. She is worse than the "white trash" she abhors. She is a "wart hog from hell," a person whose constant need to reassure herself of her worthiness is testimony of how, down deep, she knows herself to be terribly unworthy.

So at the fence of the pig parlor, Mrs. Turpin, a considerably reduced person, calls out into the gathering dark, seeking some response to her misery. She looks at the pigs, as if looking into the core of mystery; she looks and listens as if receiving some ultimate life-giving knowledge. There is a "visionary light" amid the grunting and rutting of the pigs. She sees a vast bridge, swung from earth up to heaven:

> Upon it a vast horde of souls were rumbling toward heaven. There were whole companies of white-trash, clean for the first time in their lives, and bands of blacks in white robes, and battalions of freaks and lunatics shouting and clapping and leaping like frogs. And bringing up the end of the procession was a tribe of people who she recognized at once as those who, like herself and Claud, had always had a little of everything. . . . They were marching behind the others with great dignity, accountable as they had always been for good order and common sense and respectable behavior. . . . Yet she could see by their shocked faces that even their virtues were being burned away.

Even their virtues are burned away. They have nothing, even those who thought they had something, except the gracious embrace of a God who calls them up to his kingdom. All those whom Mrs. Turpin has scorned are ahead of her, and she and Claud, now stripped of their virtues, dance at the end of the procession.

The story ends therefore with a second revelation. The first is the revelation of judgment in the girl's accusation and the book hurled at Mrs. Turpin. Now, with her alleged "virtues" having been burned away, Mrs. Turpin is made clean, ready for a second revelation, a vision by the pig parlor, a vision which ends with her hearing "the voices of the souls climbing upward into the starry field and shouting hallelujah."

How often we, like Mrs. Turpin, see ourselves as somewhat above the general procession of humanity. "I may not be the best person in the world, but at least I am better than so-and-so." We build up ourselves by putting down others. We tell ourselves that we know where we are, know what step to take next, where we are placed on the ladder of social class. Then, if we are lucky, there comes some devastating moment of revelation in which we, looking with superiority upon some other whom we presume to be beneath us, are made honestly to see ourselves.

Must Flannery O'Connor be so severe with us? Is it necessary for her to sketch our situation in such harsh tones? Why must we be forced, by a story like this one, to stare into the brutal mirror of honesty?

Christians live by the conviction that honesty is impossible, that our truthful selves are irretrievable without some means of telling our story in a truthful way. Repentance does not come naturally. It involves learning a story and practicing moves which are not part of American life in general.

What we need, in order to be truthful, is some means of facing the facts without either hating ourselves for our past or hating those who remind us of it. How can we be free?

As Christians we are told that our redemption comes (in Stanley Hauerwas' words) "by being formed by a truthful narrative that helps us appreciate the limits and possibilities of those stories we have not chosen but are part and parcel of who we are."[1]

Christians are answerable to a story which says that God forgives us—even from the cross, forgives us. This divine willingness to take us back is not based upon some sort of cheap graciousness; a cross is not cheap. Christian forgiveness does not say that our sin is inconsequential or forgettable. Rather, forgiveness begins in God's amazing determination to have a family, in God's relentless pursuit of us even into the wilderness.

This helps to explain why, to the end, O'Connor thought of herself as a very Christian writer. Her Catholicism was integral to her way of construing the world. She really demonstrates that we are saved by grace. We are, all of us, once our prentensions are peeled away, "wart hogs from hell." How can we be, in the words of Mrs. Turpin, both "hogs" and "saved"?

If God is not willing to save sinners, then on the basis of O'Connor's depiction of human nature, we are damned. In her

1. Hauerwas, "A Tale of Two Stories," p. 29.

stories, moral superiority is never an option. Programs for human
betterment are not a possibility. Our virtues, like those of Mrs.
Turpin, are a sham. We are doomed. The folk who people her
world are crazy, freakish, without the ability to lift up themselves.

And these are the ones for whom Christ died. O'Connor
demonstrates her conviction that we are saved by grace. This is
never of our own doing. We are too crazy, too deceitful for that.
Only God could help us. Only a crucified God who forgave us
could possibly love freaks like us. And God does.

O'Connor is able to be so unflinchingly honest because she is
so utterly convinced of the sure and certain grace of God. Grace
precedes honesty. Only because she knows a story of a God who
came to us, embraced us, and forgave us, can she honestly tell
stories about who we really are.

Sitting on her mother's sofa in Milledgeville, Georgia, staring
at us, knowing that she was dying of painful lupus, the disease
which killed her father and would strike her down early as well,
O'Connor looked at us with such intensity and honesty. My
friend at Duke, novelist Reynolds Price, says of Flannery O'Connor, "She has a mean streak in her." Her tough humor strikes
many as mean-spirited and even cruel. Yet, in an age of lies and
self-derived dignity, I find her stories to be a splash of honest,
cold water in the face of my presumption.

Humor tends to deal with the incongruities of life. In those all
too rare moments when we are made honestly to look at ourselves,
the incongruity can be especially great. The gap between our lovingly
polished, idealized self-image and the reality of our selves can be vast.

Someone has said that, humor, laughter at our faults and
foibles, gives us the gift of seeing ourselves as God sees us.
Looking at that great gap between our shaky self-esteem and the
grubby realities of who we really are, surely God must smile. Let
us hope, that in evaluating each of us, God has a sense of humor!

I keep a copy of O'Connor's stories by my bedside and turn to
it from time to time. We pastors must function much of the time in
what the psychotherapist Jung called the *persona*. The persona was
the mask which actors in Greek drama wore during a play. One

character might play many different roles. By changing the mask, the persona, a character changed personality. Jung defined the *persona* as that polished exterior which we present to other people, our idealized, public self. Pastors must function much of the time with a rather well-polished, bright persona, always being kind, patient, and caring with others. Jung taught that the brighter the "persona," the darker the shadow underneath, the "shadow" being that real self which we often hide from public view.

When I read O'Connor, as a pastor, as someone with a rather well-polished public exterior, it is for me an exercise in confession, always a painful, though invigorating look at myself and that on which my positive self-image is based. I find myself stripped naked before the relentless, uncompromising gaze of this woman, this writer who describes us in such cold, direct, dispassionate detail. I say to myself, "I am not at all accustomed to honesty. I lie. I do not know my own self."

To know why such moments of painful honesty are called "religious," one would have to know another story. It is a story of one who was whipped, scorned, lynched by a proud, dishonest world. It is a story of a crucified God who, in horrible deformity, nailed to a cross, stared down upon us in our bloody, lying, freakishness and still was able to embrace us, to say, even to freaks like us, "Sisters and brothers, I love you still."

For Further Reflection

1. What concrete acts of repentance and conversion might you perform in order to participate in Christ's work related to racism in America?

2. What is the most honest moment you have experienced with Christ?

3. In what ways does Sunday worship offer you opportunity to take a look at yourself from the standpoint of divine judgment and grace?

6

On Our Way
to Hell

Love in the Ruins

He who sits in the heavens laughs; the LORD has them in derision.

—Psalm 2:4

Psalm 2 says that God sits in the heavens and laughs at us. Let's hope so. According to the works of Southern, Catholic writer, Walker Percy, there is much about us which amuses. Psalm 2 is about the only place laughter is mentioned in the Old Testament (except for Sarah's obstetrical laughter in Genesis 18:12 , which is also a laughter of mockery). God's laughter in Psalm 2 is mocking, scornful derision. Some readers don't like Walker Percy, finding his brand of humor too full of scorn to be funny. Yet scorn is legitimate laughter, perhaps even (according to Psalm 2) a faithful response to human weaknesses or divine workings.

It is July 4, 1983. We are on the brink of George Orwell's predicted apocalypse, 1984. This is the setting of Walker Percy's 1971 novel, *Love in the Ruins.* We are hunkered down in a grove of pine trees, on the edge of a ruined cloverleaf at the interstate highway with a loaded carbine in hand. Our guide into this disintegrating world of North American meltdown is Dr. Thomas More, American namesake of the Renaissance humanist-saint:

> Now in these dread latter days of the old violent beloved U.S.A. and of the Christ-forgetting Christ-haunted death-dealing Western world I came to myself. . . . Either I am right and a catastrophe will occur, or it won't and I'm crazy. In either case the outlook is not so good.

The phrase, "I came to myself" has got to be an allusion, not only to Luke 17:17 but also to Dante's *Inferno* where, at the midlife, Dante says, "I came to myself within a dark wood where the straight way was lost." Just as midlife was for Dante, Tom More is lost, with a whole nation on its way to hell in late-twentieth century USA. And the dark will be very dark indeed.

We're at the end. "God has at last removed his blessing from the U.S.A." There is fighting in the streets, war between the rich and the poor, the "principalities and powers are everywhere victorious" and the whole world is dying for want of a good repairman.

The Church? Don't look for much guidance or consolation there. The American church in *Love in the Ruins* has been fractured into "the American Catholic Church whose new Rome is Cicero, Illinois." Its main beliefs are property values and the neighborhoods. *The Star-Spangled Banner* is sung at the elevation of the Host at its Eucharist.

Then there are the Dutch schismatics whose priests marry and who "believe in relevance but not God."

Finally, there is the Roman Catholic remnant which is "a tiny scattered flock with no place to go."

As for the Protestants, they have mostly been done in by the televison evangelists. Protestant churches now specialize in golf tournaments which are promoted with banners reading, "Jesus Christ, the Greatest Pro of Them All."

Politically, the old Republicans have become the new Knothead Party whose slogan is, "No man can be too knotheaded in the service of his country." They are big into school prayer and birth-control programs for Africa, Asia, and Alabama.

The Democrats, on the other hand, are now reformed into the LEFTPAPASANE party whose acronym stands for Liberty, Equality, Fraternity, The Pill, Atheism, Pot, Antipollution, Sex, Abortion Now, and Euthanasia.

Buzzards circle overhead. The scientist-narrator speaks sarcastically of a world which once believed that "there is nothing wrong with the world that couldn't be set right by controlling germs and human wastes." Thus *Love in the Ruins* is a dark, dark world becoming unglued, not because of the anger of God but of human silliness.

The dark, sardonic humor in many of Percy's novels perhaps arises from Percy's own past. There is much gloom in Percy's past: his father committed suicide; his mother died in an automobile accident. During the early 1940s, Percy contracted tuberculosis while working as a pathologist in New York. A promising young physician, now confined for five years to bed during a long and frustrating recuperation from tubuerculosis, Percy began to read our old friend, Dostoyevsky. This reading led Percy for the first time to question his naive faith in science, his American hope for the basic goodness of modernity, and drove him into psychotherapy.

Percy left the practice of medicine and became a writer. He converted to Catholicism in 1947. Critics debate how Percy's Catholicism affects his writing. I believe that Catholicism led Percy to a critique of his native Southern humanism (bred into him by his remarkable farmer-writer uncle, William Alexander Percy) and to a searing questioning of the pretensions of modern secularity. More importantly, his Catholicism fostered his pervasive faith that, in the end, the grace of God overcomes all, even human silliness.

One need not expect too much plot in Percy's novels. At times, he explains too much rather than narrates. His novels tend to be in the form of fictionalized essays in which Percy (or those characters who embody his voice) does most of the talking. Always he is a physician, a doctor staring at our nakedness, picking over our bodies and souls with a straightforward, critical eye, then straightforwardly reporting what he sees.

Early in his work, Percy pondered why it is that the material-istic modern western world appears to have given us so much, yet we feel so empty, so forlorn, even amid such plenty. The nar-rator of *Love in the Ruins* lives in a place called "Paradise Estates," where the rich are armed and dug in against the poor, where the poor roam as armed bands of revolutionaries in a land where "wolves have been seen in downtown Cleveland, like Rome during the Black Plague." Some paradise. Tom More laments that, in America, you are free to buy anything you want, but you can't get it fixed.

In an early essay, Percy noted a sometimes desperate, usually ill-defined sense of homelessness among us:

> Why is a man apt to feel bad in a good environ-ment, say suburban Short Hills, New Jersey, on an ordinary Wednesday afternoon? Why is the same man apt to feel good in a very bad environment, say an old hotel on Key Largo during a hurricane?
>
> Why is it that a man riding a good commuter train from Larchmont to New York, whose needs and dri-ves are satisfied, who has a good home, loving wife and family, good job, who enjoys unprecedented "cultural and recreational facilities," often feels bad without knowing why?
>
> Why is the good life which men have achieved in the twentieth century so bad that only news of world catastrophes, assassinations, plane crashes, mass mur-ders, can divert one from the sadness of ordinary mornings?
>
> What does a man do when he finds himself living after an age has ended and he can no longer under-stand himself because the theories of the new age are not yet known, and so everything is upside down, people feeling bad when they should feel good, good when they should feel bad?
> —*The Message in the Bottle*, pp. 4–7

Science implies that we are, despite ourselves, making progress, and humanism suggests that we are, despite momentary setbacks, good at heart. Percy will have none of it. We are lost in the cosmos, adrift, cut loose from former ersatz consolations. If all our accumulated stuff won't save us or bring us home, what (or who) will?

Tom More drinks many Gin Fizzes, and they offer some deadening of the pain that is constantly, but inchoately, felt. Yet the alcohol wears off or is required in increasing quantities. Eventually, reality sets in with sobriety.

Most of his fiction is a searing denunciation of what Percy calls our "scientific humanism," that bogus faith that humanity has within itself the resources for digging out of our present predicament. Percy's protagonist in *Love in the Ruins* treats a strange malady in his patients known as "Angelism." We so want to be godlets unto ourselves. Elsewhere, in another novel, people are in the grip of what Percy calls "The Thanatos Syndrome," the walking, half-waking dead. The left and the right, politically or religiously, are both cut from the same cloth. They are mere mirror images of one another, just different species of the same genus— scientific humanism run amuck. Gods we are not.

And yet, in *Love in the Ruins,* Percy indicts us with wit, sarcasm, and visionary invective. On a visit to a medical school in its last days, More says,

> Students are, if the truth be known, a bad lot. En masse they're as fickle as a mob, manipulable by any professor who'll stoop to it. They have, moreover, an infinite capacity for repeating dull truths and old lies with all the insistence of self-discovery. Nothing is drearier than the ideology of students, left or right.

God is a problem for nearly all of Percy's people because we've lost the capacity for real joy, or real pain, therefore real guilt or real love. Toward the end of the novel, as the good old USA disintegrates and cities burn, Tom More staggers into a Catholic confessional:

"Bless me, Father, for I have sinned," I say and fall silent, forgetting everything.

"When was your last confession?" asks the priest patiently.

"Eleven years ago."

Another groan escapes the priest. Again he peeps at his watch. . . .

"Father, I can make my confession in one sentence."

"Good," says the priest, cheering up.

"I do not recall the number of occasions, Father, but I accuse myself of drunkenness, lusts, envies, fornication, delight in the misfortunes of others, and loving myself better than God and other men."

"I see," says the priest, who surprises me by not looking surprised. Perhaps he's just sleepy. "Do you have contrition and a firm purpose of amendment?"

"I don't know."

"You don't know? You don't feel sorry for your sins?"

"I don't feel much of anything". . .

"You are aware of your sins, you confess them, but you are not sorry for them?"

"That is correct."

"Why?"

"I couldn't say."

"Pity."

"I'm sorry."

"You are?"

"Yes."

"For what?"

"For not being sorry."

Even our sins are more silly than tragic. What's to become of us?

His indictment against the late twentieth century is set against a background of Percy's conviction that we are, despite ourselves, on a pilgrimage back to God. In hell we may be, but it is more a purgatory than a hell, a trek back toward the God whom we thought we had overcome. In a fit of passion for a voluptuous nurse, Tom More realizes that he is hankering after God even more than beautiful women. He blurts out to himself, to God, to whomever,

"I prayed, arms stretched out like a Mexican, tears streaming down my face. Dear God, I can see it now, why can't I see it at other times, that it is you I love in the beauty of the world and in all the lovely girls and dear good friends, and it is pilgrims we are, wayfarers on a journey, and not pigs, nor angels."

Wayfarers, pilgrims, all on a journey. Neither pointless pigs or adorable angels, we are sinners, yet also recipients of grace, great grace, all the more great because God offers it to us. It is not that we are heroic searchers after the truth. In Percy's fiction, we are creatures of a God who subtly lures us, reaches out to us, speaks to us even though we are often tone deaf to the divine allurements. Thomas More, despite himself, ends the novel somewhere in the arms of God, safe, at last at rest, entwined in the limbs of his wife Ellen, all evidence in the chaotic world to the contrary, "at home in bed where all good folk belong." Even amid the ruins, love.

If novelists like Updike or Dostoyevsky see our sin as dark demonstration of our fallenness, then a Catholic Southern novelist like O'Connor or Percy sees sin as opportunity for God to show God's great mercy. God smiles rather than damns. In the end, there is no hope for us, pitiful as we are, nothing except for smiling mercy.

For Further Reflection

1. Where do we Christians muster the truth to be honest about our current situation? Is honesty dependent upon an experience of a gracious God?

2. It is possible only to wring our hands and weep over the breakdown of late twentieth century America. Or we can laugh. How is laughter closer to faith than tears?

3. What responsibility do Christians have to care for the plight of the nation and nations surrounding us?

4. How has God sought you in your life?

7

The Soul in Sloth

In the Beauty of the Lilies

All is vanity. What do people gain from all the toil at which they toil under the sun? A generation goes, and a generation comes.

—Ecclesiastes 1:2-4

In his epic account of his life, *The Education of Henry Adams*, Henry Adams describes the dissipation of religion from his soul:

> Of all the conditions of his youth which afterwards puzzled the grown-up man, this disappearance of religion puzzled him most. The boy went to church twice every Sunday; he was taught to read his Bible, and he learned religious poetry by heart; he believed in a mild deism; he prayed, he went through all the forms; but neither to him nor to his brothers or sisters was religion real. . . . they all threw it off at the first possible moment, and never afterwards entered a church. The religious instinct had vanished, and could not be revived, although one made in later life many efforts to recover it. . . . The faculty of turning away one's eyes as one approaches a chasm is not unusual.[1]

1. Henry Adams, *The Education of Henry Adams* (New York: Random House, Modern Books, 1931), p. 34.

That's the way the loss of faith was for proper Bostonian Brahmin, Henry Adams. Faith, ebbed away, without rage or passionate resistance, politely, slowly, but steadily until that day when faith was no more. One turns away the eyes from the emptiness within and the darkness without and goes on.

The ebb of faith was something like that for the Reverend Clarence Wilmot, a chief character in John Updike's *In the Beauty of the Lilies*, though other generations of the Wilmot family find other forms of faith in this novel.

The modern world is said to be a world emptied of mystery, devoid of belief. As a pastor, I've seen two types of disbelief. There is that lonely, rather heroic disbelief which comes at the end of a long, tortured journey of the soul, the result of logic unmoved, or a hurt too deep to heal. When, in *The Blood of the Lamb*, Don Wanderhope says he disbelieves, we know it is deep, frustrated anger at God's refusal to be God on our terms which is called "disbelief." We can understand that form of troubled God relationship.

The other type of disbelief is noble, understandable, quite forgivable, I think. One person told me that she could not believe in God, despite her attempts. Her beloved daughter had died at the age of five. As she left the hospital that bleak afternoon, her belief left her.

I believe that God grieves with such unbelief, rather than rages against it. It is unbelief akin to Jesus' own, "My God, my God, why hast thou forsaken me?" from the cross (Matt. 27:46, KJV).

When Jesus cried thus, he was quoting from Psalm 22. The Psalms, Job, and Ecclesiastes, speak of that disbelief borne out of anger at the world, anger and frustration that God is not God in the way in which we think God ought to be God. That such unbelief receives such eloquent expression in scripture itself is, to me, testimony to its sacredness.

More common, in every sense of that word, is disbelief of the modern sort which comes from a failure of intellectual nerve, the slothful unwillingness to investigate, to launch out, to risk. It is not so much atheism as it is a kind of limp agnosticism. It is disbelief on the order of my disbelief in rugby. When asked by our chapel sound technician, "Don't you think rugby is just great?" I replied, "I've seen it once from afar, never played it, never will. It seems silly to me, but I just don't know."

When asked about the demise of the modern novel, Flannery O'Connor replied,

> People without hope not only don't write novels, but what is more to the point, they don't read them. They don't take long looks at anything, because they lack the courage. The way to despair is to refuse to have any kind of experience, and the novel, of course, is a way to have experience.[2]

Modern people "don't take long looks at anything," says O'Connor, not necessarily because we are intellectually lazy, which we surely are, but because we "lack the courage." Darkness immobilizes, and it is possible, as a kind of defense, to move from feeling bad to not feeling at all.

I thought of O'Connor's judgment after finishing John Updike's *In the Beauty of the Lilies.*

The novel exudes apathy, passivity. I have always found Updike's style appealing. His extravagant, verbose, detached way of dealing with matters, mostly upper middle class and sexual matters, has seemed to me just right. Yet when he explicitly deals with religion, we are reminded that faith requires a certain amount of passion, perhaps more than even the passion required for sex. Certainly it requires courage, and courage seems to be a commodity in which Updike believes we are deficient.

Lilies chronicles the decline of an American family, beginning in a Presbyterian manse in Paterson, New Jersey, ending with a

---

2. Johnathan Franze, "Perchance to Dream: In the Age of Images, A Reason to Write Novels," *Harpers* (April 1996): 53.

cult holocaust in Colorado reminiscent of the demise of the Branch Davidians in Waco, Texas.

Clarence Wilmot is a Princeton-educated preacher whose faith gradually ebbs away. When his scholarly Calvinism is spent, Wilmot is left with nothing with which to do business with the Almighty. Did Calvinism conceive a God so high, lifted up and remote that one day Calvin's heirs awoke to discover no one was there? More probably, nineteenth century Protestant liberalism attempted to make moral and missionary activity substitute for mystery and revelation (much as many mainliner Protestants now do) and woke up one day with nothing but "God's inexorable recession."

It's all rather sad. But there's nothing to be done about it. Resignation is the only option. The modern world arrogantly presents itself not as a point of view to be debated, a perspective which can be argued for or against, but rather as a fact to which we must adjust. That other "worlds" might be possible is simply not acknowledged as possible by the modern world. Everything else is labeled fantasy, wishful thinking, unrealistic, naive.

The modern world began, in great part, as a ruthless search for "the facts." Descartes sought certitude. He loved mathematics for its alleged certainty and hoped to make philosophy as certain a science. This was the promise of the scientific method. Here was a procedure whereby we would strip ourselves bare of our passions, our prejudices and commitments and get down to THE FACTS. Here was an epistemology, a method of knowledge, based upon positivism, whereby humanity would at last arise out of that murky swamp inhabited by values and opinions and faith and stand on the solid, non-negotiable, undebatable ground of THE FACTS. Serene, nonconflicted, self-evident knowledge was to be the gift of modern ways of knowing.

Did not Thomas Jefferson, that supremely modern man, begin his Declaration of Independence with the assertion that, "We hold these truths to be self-evident that. . . ." That's the truth the modern world wants, truth which is self-evident, available to all without risk, or journey, or cost, or conflict. Truth, free-standing, nonconflicted FACTS.

So the modern world dispenses with God, for there is no room in our closed modern epistemologies for knowledge which is derived from means other than through our own rules for knowing. Reverend Wilmot bows before the fact of God's demise. He doesn't protest or whine. Rather, he resigns himself to THE FACTS.

The best for which spent Calvinism can hope, in Wilmot, is stoic resignation before a now silent, baffling universe. He does not argue, or rage, or struggle against the advent of night. The former Reverend Wilmot, now peddling encyclopedias door-to-door—volumes of detached, pointless knowledge—to poor people in Paterson who need jobs more than facts, is an image of modern humanity. Modernity began, we have said, as a search for THE FACTS.

The encyclopedic collection, arrangement, and compilation of the facts gave birth to such supremely modern achievements as the computer. "We are waiting for more data to come in," we say, in explanation for our inactivity. In his book, *Technopoly,* Neil Postman says that we don't need more facts. We already have more information than we can use. What we are dying for is lack of courage, vision, hope, dreams—all things which no computer can deliver. Failing at courage, we simply assemble more facts. Detailed, well organized, collected, but alas, mostly pointless knowledge—the encyclopedia—is us.

Updike writes, "In his present state he was a husk, depleted. . . ."

Wilmot becomes the modern, educated American for whom resigned disbelief is presented as an intellectual achievement.

Standing up straight, on his own two feet, Wilmot no longer has to struggle with "Jehovah and His pet Israelites, that bloody tit-for-tat of the Atonement, the whole business of condemning poor fallible men and women to eternal Hell for a few mistakes in their little lifetimes, the notion in any case that our spirits can survive. . . ."

The notion that God might choose a people, in a specific time and place, to save the whole world is thus dismissed as

"Jehovah and His pet Israelites." The modern world wants universals, timeless, large truth rather than specific, peculiar, historically conditioned truth. Thus anti-Semitism, though the scourge of the ages, has been particularly vicious in our century. When these Jews did not become "modern people," as defined by the leaders of the modern nation state, when they clung to their "tribalistic" ways, they had to be killed. There is a darker side to our Enlightenment universalism. It is not by chance that the modern, enlightened Reverend Wilmot has contempt for "His pet Israelites."

Curiously, Wilmot is almost relieved after he at last admits that he no longer believes. "Oblivion became a singular comforter," says Updike. Now Wilmot, former pastor, former believer, former scholar, half-hearted encyclopedia salesman, is at rest, secure in the knowledge of the "dismal hopelessness of human life." He dies quietly, slipping into the dark, "like an unmoored boat on an outgoing tide."

Why so peaceful, why at rest?

For if, as Updike appears to believe, there is no believing, if God is *Deus absconditus* at best, only a projection of our overwrought imaginations at worst, dwelling only in some remote poetic "beauty of the lilies," "born across the sea" (my interpretation of Updike's title), then we are free. Lonely, yes; clueless, yes, but free, at rest.

There is a rest which comes from receiving what our hearts desire. There is also rest which comes from having learned to stifle desire. Updike's characters are passionate about nothing but sex, the major modern substitute for God, because they have lost desire for anything more interesting.

Evelyn Waugh called sloth a primary late-modern sin.[3] What is sloth? Lying too long in the bath? Sloth, deadliest of the seven deadly sins, is not mere laziness. It is *acedia*, apathy toward the good, indifference toward that which makes life worth living.

3. William R. May, *A Catalogue of Sins*. Quoted by Ralph C. Wood, *The Christian Century* (April 24, 1996): 457.

A Christian theologian says of the sin of sloth, "The soul in this state [sloth] is beyond mere sadness and melancholy. It has removed itself from the rise and fall of feelings; the very root of its feelings in desire is dead. That is why, for the medieval moralist, sloth was . . . the most terrifying of sins. It is sin at its uttermost limit. To be a man is to desire. The good man desires God and other things in God. The sinful man desires things in the place of God, but he is still recognizably human, inasmuch as he has known desire. The slothful man, however, is a dead man, an arid waste. . . . his desire itself has dried up."[4]

Ralph Wood defines sloth as "spiritual dryness and deadness of the soul that has lost its hunger for God."[5] It is this arid indifference which is meant by the term *sloth*.

Of the ex-Reverend Wilmot's son, Teddy, spent-belief's child of the modern age, Updike says that nothing made Teddy Wilmot "indignant. He was a man at peace, still curious about the world but with never any hope of changing it. . . . Teddy had no faith to offer; he had only the facts of daily existence."

Yes, the facts.

As far as I can tell, this is about the best Updike sees for us. Not the heroic struggle found in Homer, or the peaceful, enlightened resignation into the hands of the God of Dostoyevsky. Rather, it is the urbane, unperturbed defeat of the late twentieth century agnostic. The agnostic is the one who says not, "I don't believe," but more modestly, "I don't know." What we do not know about the agnostic is whether or not this is agnosticism born out of intellectual humility or out of sloth, intellectual laziness, failure to risk, to journey forth, to commit. I think with Updike it is the latter.

The progeny of the Reverend Wilmot find some reason for living. A daughter loses herself in the materialistic and sexual fantasies of Hollywood. The son settles down into the comforts of a quiet, middle-class marriage. And the picture of our

4. Wood, p. 457.
5. Wood, p. 457.

age grows more clear. Faith becomes not faith in the God of Israel but rather some vague, vapid, deeply sentimental drivel about "the beauty of the lilies" out somewhere across the sea, remote from us, so remote a journey, and at such a cost, we dare not risk.

It is a world I once admired. When I first met the preacher of Ecclesiastes, he seemed bracing in his honesty:

> I saw all the deeds that are done under the sun; and see, all is vanity and a chasing after wind. . . . I said to myself, "I have acquired great wisdom, surpassing all who were over Jerusalem before me; and my mind has had great experience of wisdom and knowledge." And I applied my mind to know wisdom and to know madness and folly. I perceived that this also is but a chasing after wind.
> —Ecclesiastes 1:14, 16-17

Note that everything here is in monologue. There is no conversation with any other outside the self. The self looks upon the world and stands in sovereign judgment upon it. "I said to myself . . . " No one is addressed outside the self. All is in vain. There is nothing but wind. Why bother?

Heroic, intellectually honest resignation? Or sloth? The lives produced by this mode of thinking may not be that interesting; certainly they are in no way heroic, as Updike's rather long novel shows. But at least they are at rest, at peace, having quit the battle, having retired to the tending of their own middle-class gardens, having nothing more to say to God, having no expectation of being addressed by anything or anyone outside themselves.

And the picture of late twentieth century America, upper middle-class suburban Yuppiedom grows more clear. In fact, the sort of disbelieving which Updike depicts here is decidedly class connected. Richard John Neuhaus interprets Updike as the major commentator on the faith lapse of the privileged:

Over the years, Updike has presented himself as
someone who, like most Americans of his class, has
misplaced his faith and wishes he could find it again
but knows he can't. In Updike's view, the ineluctable
disappearance of religion in the life of Americans has
been replaced by the ersatz religions of devotion to
the bitch goddess of material success, and to the
excitements of a degraded popular culture. . . .[6]

Neuhaus implies that this manner of disbelief has not been
the experience of most Americans, only the most bored and
affluent. What Updike seems to want is a posture without rage,
where no emotional life is desired beyond the momentary release
provided by sex, where God is not so much denied as not pub-
licly discussed.

So Neuhaus dismisses *In The Beauty of the Lilies* as providing
only "a momentary pleasure of pretended angst about the certi-
tudes [of modern people], a brush with ever so refined and
regretful unbelief."

It is of the nature of modernity to be arrogant, to believe that
we are privileged to live at the summit of human development.
We stand in judgment upon everything and everyone who preceded us. Yet, as we have noted, there is a long tradition in
scripture, at least as old as Ecclesiastes, of nihilism, of critical
struggle with God. Perhaps the ex-Reverend Wilmot's story suggests that disbelief here in affluent, late twentieth century America is a particular form of apathy, of sloth, *acedia.*

Philosophers have noted the development of what they call
the "onlooker consciousness" in modernity. We are trained to
cultivate that stance toward the world which presumes detach-
ment, objectivity, distance between subject and object. "Want to
know about the frog?"

"First, kill the frog. Split him down the middle, take out his
innards, label the parts. There. We've explained the frog."

6. "The Pleasures of Regretful Unbelief," *First Things* (June/July 1996): 63.

Someone objects, "But we killed the frog."

True, there are some unfortunate byproducts of the modern way of knowing. So H.G. Wells complained, "There was a time when I gazed upon the stars with great wonder. Now I look at a starry night as I look upon faded wallpaper in a railway station waiting room."

Having transformed God from a relationship, a friend, though often a troubling friend, into an object for investigation, having set up the requirements for God to meet if God is to be worshiped as our God, many awoke toward the end of the twentieth century to find that it was as if God had faded into the wallpaper. This we have called "losing our faith."

For the heirs of the ex-Reverend Wilmot, there is now nothing much in which to believe, to have convictions about, to live or to die for except perhaps Hollywood.

My friend Richard Lischer, in his book on the preaching of Martin Luther King, Jr., noted that, in the predominately white church, we have been trained by biblical studies of the past few decades to understand scripture by disciplining ourselves to step back from scripture, to strip ourselves of our prejudices and preconceptions, to divest ourselves of any commitments, in other words to adopt the "onlooker consciousness" in regard to the biblical text. The results of such sterile reading of scripture are all around us.

In the African-American church, on the other hand, the tendency with the Bible has been to step into the text, to try to text on for size, to identify with the various characters of the story, to put oneself in the places of the protagonists. Only such passionate reading, such performance of scripture, enabled the black church to survive the assaults of a racist world.

I therefore read *In the Beauty of the Lilies* as a saga of twentieth century American disbelief, the piteous disengagement from the struggle with God, a depiction of the flotsam and jetsam of late capitalist culture.

Visiting on our campus, Tony Campolo, the evangelical activist, was asked by one of our conservative, evangelical students what Bible-believing Christians might do to counter some of the sexual promiscuity on our campus.

"What can born again, Bible-believing Christians do in the face of campus sexual promiscuity?" Campolo asked. "You can get down on your knees and ask God to forgive you for being so boring that nobody has come to Christ because of you!"

"I mean that," he continued. "People, we are in the love business. Pascal was right. Faith is a matter of passion, *passion*, love, anger, heat and all that. Go easy on modern pagans. All they've got is sex. We've got the God of Israel, which is much more interesting than sex. But we work with what we've got."

Updike tells the saga of the Wilmots with such skill and charm that we are likely to sympathize with them, to sentimentalize their lapse into urbane disbelief, without recognizing their tragedy. But the novel is a tragedy of those who refuse to rage against the night. Disbelief ought to be made of sterner stuff.

For Further Reflection

1. What are the spiritual disciplines you employ in order to keep passionate your relationship to Christ?

2. What are, for you, the greatest challenges to faith?

3. Many modern people say they no longer feel close to God. Is that due to God's absence or our own absence? How might we help others be open to God's presence?

8

Suffer the Little Children

The Blood of the Lamb

> Worthy is the Lamb that was slaughtered . . . . to the
> Lamb be blessing and honor and glory and might for-
> ever and ever!
> —Revelation 5:12, 13

"I find it difficult to believe in a good God when there is so much innocent suffering in the world," she said. The implication was that she was so sensitive to the suffering of others, so finely tuned morally, that the thought of a good God mixed up with a messed up world like ours was well, unbelievable. Aside from the implied arrogance of her assertion ("I am more sensitive to the suffering of others than any possible god might be."), Stanley Hauerwas has helped me to see how framing the "question of suffering" in this way already prejudices the discussion in such a way that the God of Israel and the Church is bound to be the loser in the conversation.[1]

I have long suspected that philosophically posed questions are never the place to begin, particularly when it is a question of suffering. Theodicy, human inquiry into the justice of God, has a long history—none of it too fruitful. David Hume, in his *Dia-*

---

1. See Stanley M. Hauerwas, *God, Medicine, and Suffering* (William B. Eerdmans: Grand Rapids, Mich., 1994), pp. 1–38.

logues Concerning Natural Religion, long ago philosophically
phrased the question we have been unable satisfactorily to
answer: "Is He [God] willing to prevent evil, but not able? then
is He impotent. Is He able, but not willing? then is He malevo-
lent. Is He both able and willing? whence then is evil?"

Many of us have been conditioned, through years of school,
to begin with an assumption of what God ought to be like if
God were worthy of our belief (i.e. loving and caring, always
opposed to human suffering), and if our search for such a deity
proves futile, then to conclude that God does not exist.

But what if we start not with philosophical constructs or with
our presuppositions but rather with a story? Stories are concrete,
particular, not general and abstract. Stories have the great advan-
tage of steering fairly close to the shore, of keeping themselves
close to the hard facts of life rather than floating off into vague
abstractions. And when we are looking at or experiencing suffering, we would do well to keep close to the facts.

Nothing is more maddening than cool, dispassionate, general
discussions of other people's pain. One of the funniest, or most
infuriating passages in the Gospel of John is the disciples'
attempt to have a theological debate about the poor man born
blind in John 9:1-41. Jesus appears to have little patience with
their, "Rabbi, who sinned, this man or his parents, that he was
born blind?" (9:2)

Few novels take us more deeply into these matters than Peter
De Vries' *The Blood of the Lamb*. Having read his uproarious satire
of the liberal, compromised church, *The Mackerel Plaza,* I
expected this novel to be funny too. It is not. Where there is wit,
it is sharp and dark. But what should one expect of the story of
the death of a child? Yet the novel is more about Carol's father,
Don Wanderhope. Like many of De Vries' characters, the name is
significant. Don is the son of Dutch Calvinist immigrants whose
subservience to Reason got the best of their Faith. He says that he
grew up among folk who "thought Jesus was a Hollander." When
Don's greatly beloved older brother, Louie, dies of pneumonia,
young Don is thrown into theological confusion, asking himself

why his Calvinist forebears have worshiped a God who is "scarcely distinguishable from the devil they feared." Finally, Don cries out, "Why doesn't He pick on somebody his size?"

As a young man, Don enrolls at the University of Chicago and his life is off to a good start. Don engages in a couple of sexual experiments with young women, becomes conscious of fashion, and begins his climb up the social ladder.

His climb upward is frustrated by a (misdiagnosed) case of tuberculosis. Don is sent to a sanitorium where he befriends, and eventually makes love to, a young woman who is very sick with tuberculosis. When she dies after surgery, Don feels confirmed in his anger at, or disbelief in, God. A letter from home tells him that his father—found one night by his mother, swatting cockroaches in the kitchen with her brassiere—is going mad. Don places his father in a nursing home, thinking to himself, "There seems to be little support in reality for the popular belief that we are mellowed by suffering. Happiness mellows us, not troubles; pleasure, perhaps, even more than happiness."

Eventually, Don marries a troubled woman, Greta. Greta is consumed by guilt over a past affair. Their marriage is stormy and difficult yet yields the one bright ray of sun within Don's life —their daughter, Carol.

When Greta at last takes her own life, Don joyously loses himself in the responsibilities of raising Carol. Although he grieves for Greta, Don loves Carol with unrestrained affection, taking joy in Carol's every move. Carol even helps Don make a sort of reconciliation with God. Coaxed by their formidable maid, Mrs. Brodhag, to go to church on Christmas Eve to watch Carol participate in a candlelight service, Don feels, despite himself, "every known emotion blaze within me" as he "thanked God. . . , my daughter's warm hand in mine."

There is only a hint of presentiment when Carol falls ill. Her illness is diagnosed as a passing, unimportant infection.

"*That* was the happiest moment of my life," says Wanderhope. "We could break bread in peace again, my child and I.

The greatest experience open to man then is the recovery of the commonplace. Coffee in the morning and whiskeys in the evening again without fear."

During this lull back in normalcy, Wanderhope is asked by the editors of his college newspaper for a two-hundred words-or-less statement of his "philosophy of life." He eagerly responds with secularist drivel, presented as profundity:

> I believe that man must learn to live without those consolations called religious, which his own intelligence must by now have told him belong to the childhood of the race. . . . The quest for Meaning is foredoomed. Human life "means" nothing. . . . Man has only his two feet to stand on, his own human trinity to see him through: Reason, Courage, and Grace.

This self-confident cloak of sunny, straightforward rationality begins to unravel just a few days later when, vacationing with dear Carol in Bermuda, she falls ill and they rush back to the doctor who tells them that tests suggest leukemia.

The doctor urges Don not to be concerned, sending them to a world-renowned specialist in New York, praising the great advances made against this disease by medical science, reassuring Don that, "They're working on it day and night, and they're bound to get it soon."

The doctor promises Don that Carol will be in school in September.

In New York the acclaimed specialist speaks medical jargon and scientific gibberish to Wanderhope, citing the development of miracle drugs—antibiotics, chemotherapy, steroids—yet interspersing his talk with hints about "things getting tricky" with Carol's illness.

It is at this point in the novel that Don's name begins to become revelatory—Wanderhope. Don is desperate, clinging to any shred of hope, terrified out of his wits. The once self-assured secularist is beginning to crumble, we suspect. He has been cast adrift from his confident, comfortable atheism. But that does not mean that he has lost faith, given up on hope; rather, it means that Don is shifting hope. Now his faith is wandering toward the sterile temples of medicine and their white-coated priests.

"Do you believe in God as well as play at him?" Don asks the cancer specialist. Is Don being his usual cynical self, or is his question a cry of hope? Does this doctor know and control as much as he would have us think? Can he, like some god, set things right in a world now so horribly out of kilter?

The doctor replies that, with his hours in the lab, and his trips to hospitals all over the country, "I have no time to think about such matters."

Now begins Don's descent with Carol into the Nighttown of illness. Carol's body is repeatedly pierced by the instruments of alleged healing. In the corridors of this hospital, Don glimpses the "Slaughter of the Innocents," the crippled, emaciated, bandaged, bleeding children. He calls it "the hell of a prolonged farewell," the doctors and technicians he sees as "vampires," dressed in "butchers coats."

It is not a pretty picture, one painted with such realism, perhaps such cynicism, that it makes for difficult reading. One of the reasons De Vries cannot be recommended reading to everyone is this section of the novel.

As a young pastor, I went with an older pastor into the corridors of Henrietta Eggleston Hospital at Emory University to visit a child in our congregation who was dying with cancer. As I moved down the hall toward the ward, I became conscious that my colleague was not walking next to me. There he was, slumped over a chair near the door. I ran back toward him. His face was ashen. He was gasping for breath.

"You go on," he said. "I can't take it. I can't stand to see the suffering of children."

Any person with a simpleminded affirmation of the "goodness of life" or who affirms the educational or moral value of suffering needs to read this portion of De Vries. C. S. Lewis' pompous declaration that pain is God's megaphone to get our attention wilts when confronted with the surplus of meaningless suffering in De Vries' leukemia ward. In this "slice of hell," as Don calls it, the only truths which seem sustainable are "rage and despair."

Wanderhope wanders one day into St. Catherine's Church nearby the hospital where he prostrates himself before the shrine to St. Jude, "Patron of Lost Causes and Hopeless Cases," begging, on his knees begging, bargaining, "Give us a year. We will spend it as we have the last, missing nothing," he says in his sentimental, slobbering, pitiful prayer.

Don is given a temporary, almost cruel respite through the offices of some experimental wonder drug. Carol rallies and the doctor says that Don can take her home. Old Mrs. Brodhag bakes a cake for Don to take to the hospital for Carol's birthday celebration as she departs for home. On his way to the hospital Don, cake in hand, pauses for a grateful prayer at St. Catherine's.

The dogs of terror will not be kept at bay for long. A nurse, come to say her prayers as well at St. Catherine's, tells Don that Carol has taken a sudden turn for the worse. Don rushes to Carol's bedside. There, one look at her tells her that, "Her foul enemy had his will of her at last."

At the end, Don blesses his dear daughter, "The Lord bless thee, and keep thee: The Lord make his face shine upon thee, and be gracious unto thee: The Lord lift up his countenance upon thee, and give thee peace." He touches the holes in her skin where the needles had been inserted, seeing them as "stigmata," prints of the crucifixion. Carol manages a faint smile, the same smile she offered when her homework was done or she had successfully finished writing a poem. Carol dies, borne "on a wave that broke and crashed beyond our sight."

Don staggers out of the hospital and into a bar where he drinks himself into a stupor. When ordered out of the bar, he wobbles past St. Catherine's. He remembers that, in his rush out of the church, he left Carol's cake there. He retrieves the cake, and on his way out of the church he stops and turns toward the crucified Christ over the doorway. With all the strength left in him, Don hurls the cake at the Christ. It lands squarely beneath Christ's crown of thorns. The statue seemed to move. Christ's hands seemed patiently to remove the icing from the eyes. The icing fell in clumps on the church steps. There seemed to be a voice, "Suffer the little children to come unto me . . . for of such is the kingdom of heaven."

Wanderhope sinks to the steps. De Vries intrudes to comment, "Thus Wanderhope was found at that place which for the diabolists of his literary youth, and for those with more modest spiritual histories too, was said to be the only alternative to the muzzle of a pistol: the foot of the Cross."

If the novel had ended here, it would be an unforgettable, Dostoyevsky-type story of a man pushed to the end of his rope, a proud man finally, by the cruel workings of fate, brought to his knees at the foot of the Cross, empty-handed, broken, bereft, but curled in the arms of Providence. Wanderhope has wandered back to God, or been tethered and drawn there, or been whipped and beaten back there by the dogs of disease. There he meets a Christ who suffers with us, a Savior who saves, not by overcoming the pain but rather by entering into the pain with us. There, beneath the Cross of Jesus, Wanderhope seems to find camaraderie in his pain. There he meets not the answer to his philosophical questions but rather a God who knows what such horrible suffering means because He has been there.

But Wanderhope's journey has not yet ended. God is not done with Don, not yet. Sometime later, when the house is up for sale and Wanderhope is clearing out Carol's bedroom, he discovers a tape Carol has recorded. On the tape there is a snippet of conversation between Don and Mrs. Brodhag, then two of Carol's favorite piano pieces, then a long silence. Don almost turns off the recorder when he hears again Carol's voice. She has recorded a message for him. She reassures him that everything is all right, that he has been a great help to her. The voice is devastating. More devastation is yet to come.

Carol says on the tape that rummaging around one day she found the statement that Don had written for his college, his "philosophy of life." She says that she doesn't understand it all, but she has found it a comfort. She then reads the statement.

Imagine the crushing blow of hearing his dying daughter read back to him his own sophomoric twaddle ending with, "Man has only his own two feet to stand on, his own human trinity to see him through."

It is, for me, one of the most devastating moments in all of literature. To have our false consolations parroted back to us on the lips of a dying child—a child who, long before her time, is being made to face the finitude we are still avoiding— this, this is desolation.

Wanderhope falls to the couch, lying there for the longest time "as though I had been clubbed." He retrieves an old, cheap crucifix on a chain out of a drawer and hurls it as far as he can.

But he can't be done with the Lord represented by that cheap crucifix. De Vries has made us to wander, through the devices of this novel, with Don Wanderhope. He has taken us to hell, place of horror, locus of enlightenment the hard way. The God rendered by this novel is a tough, demanding, large, Calvinist God who does not explain nor lie with offers of cheap consolation.

De Vries is too good a storyteller, or too honest a theologian, unambiguously to tell us whether or not Don has wandered back into the arms of God. Don's escapes from Christ are fairly decisive and convincing, yet not quite. He keeps stumbling over the crucified God. Or does God keep taunting, coming back to, and harassing, trying to trip Wanderhope? Don can't really disbelieve in God. He can be angry at God, can doubt that God is "good," yet cannot believe that God is not. His Calvinist forebears wandered away from their homeland; so has Don, in his own way. He, they, were nomads, wanderers, pilgrims, immigrants. Here, in the New World, the wandering isn't over. What would "home" look like to such eternal immigrants?

Home seems to be at the foot of the cross. Yet home is not an "answer" to our deeper questions about suffering. When Don

kneels at the foot of the Cross, it is not as if he has learned
something decisive. There, beaten, whipped by life and death
Don has not received philosophical clarification, or better
answers to his questions; rather, he receives Christ, the one with
arms outstretched because they have been nailed to a cross,
Christ weeping great globs of icing tears.

As Stanley Hauerwas has convinced me in his thought on this
novel, we usually begin our ruminations about suffering with
large philosophical questions like, "How can a good God permit
there to be suffering?" We ought to begin with the specific, concrete suffering of our children. Or rather, we ought to begin not
with our standards of what God must look like if God is to be
worshipped by thoughtful, sensitive folk like us but rather with a
story, the story, the gospel of a God who comes to us as a crucified Jew from Nazareth.

Without that controlling story, we become victims of counter
stories. Wanderhope, in his terror, is willingly drawn into the
myth of modern medicine's invincibility. We can eliminate sickness by conquering disease. Sickness is a problem to be solved
scientifically. Suffering is a temporary human situation, rather
than inherent in the human condition. Suffering is a problem to
be solved rather than life to be lived. Modern people like Wanderhope fancy ourselves as cynics, skeptics, critical thinkers. Yet,
when faced with even a whiff of terror, such as the terminal illness of a child, we are almost pitifully willing to believe in anything, even the miracles of medicine.

At St. Catherine's, Don is met by (rather than meets) a God
who hangs on a cross. This is not necessarily the God we
wanted; certainly it is not the God in whom we have disbelieved.
Here is not the God who is answer to our "deeper questions."
Encounter with this God suggests that we would not even
know, in our rather silly blindness, how to frame the question
for which this God would be the answer. Most of our questions,
including even the, "How can I believe in a good God who
would allow innocent suffering?" are artful means of avoiding
being found at the foot of the Cross.

And yet *The Blood of the Lamb* suggests to me the promise (or is it the threat?) that Jesus will find us there. Sooner or later, there, at the foot of the Cross.

For Further Reflection

1. Focus upon someone you know who is suffering in mind, body, or spirit. Picture that person in your mind and pray for him or her now.

2. Before the end of this week, visit someone who is currently experiencing a time of suffering.

3. In what ways have your own experiences of suffering and pain brought you to the foot of the cross?

9

Ordinary Redemption

Saint Maybe

Be perfect, therefore, as your heavenly Father is perfect.
—Matthew 5:48

In a macabre scene in Flannery O'Connor's *Wise Blood*, wild-eyed Hazel Motes declares, "Any man with a good car don't need redemption." Shortly thereafter his wreck of a car is pushed into a pond by a sadistic deputy sheriff. The implication: everybody, especially the folk who people Flannery O'Connor's stories, needs redemption.

When Brenda Brodie made me a gift of Anne Tyler's *Saint Maybe,* she said something like, "This book will really change you, if you can get past the first hundred pages." I did and it did.

Ian Bedloe, young hero of *Saint Maybe,* is a rather typical, that is, quite ordinary, first-year college student. He has a girl-friend. He is drifting along toward adulthood.

The first part of the novel portrays how Ian's life unraveled. One night, there is a horrible shattering of his world. His beloved older brother, Danny, had married a woman, Lucy, who had two children from a previous marriage. Ian sometimes babysat for her. Where did she go when she went out at night, alone? Drawing certain conclusions from her actions, Ian became convinced that Lucy might be being unfaithful to Danny.

One night, when Lucy fails to return at the appointed hour, and Ian is kept by her tardiness from what might have been his first opportunity to sleep with his girlfriend, Ian tells his brother of his suspicions. In rage and remorse, his brother storms out and drives his car into a wall—probably a suicide. Shortly thereafter, in great grief, his brother's widow takes her own life with an overdose of sleeping pills. The children are put under the care of Ian's mother, who is clearly not up to the task of raising a new family. Ian's life is swallowed by his own feelings of guilt. Although he did not directly cause either the death of his brother, or of his brother's wife, he feels responsible. He learns that he may have been wrong in his accusations against Lucy. What if his own, possibly baseless, accusation led to this terrible chain of events in his family?

In his meanderings, Ian wanders into the storefront "Church of the Second Chance," attracted by the voices of the fifteen or so people who were singing hymns there. During the prayer time, a woman named Lula asked the church to pray for her. Lula's son, Chuckie, has just died in Vietnam, having forgotten to put on his parachute before jumping out of his plane.

Ian bursts out in laughter at the absurdity of Chuckie's stupidity. How could anybody be so dumb? The whole church turns and stares at Ian. To laugh at a grieving mother's plea for prayer seemed to Ian the worst thing he had ever done in a life in which he was lately making one wrong move after another. How could he be so dumb?

In his shame and nervousness, Ian stands up and begins to speak to the church in broken sentences:

> "I used to be good," he said. "Or I used to be not bad, at least. Not evil. I just *assumed* I wasn't evil, but lately, I don't know what's happened. Everything I touch goes wrong. I didn't mean to laugh just now. I'm sorry I laughed Mrs . . ."

Reverend Emmett, the intense, idiosyncratic pastor of The Church of the Second Chance bears down upon Ian, asking Ian if he had asked to be forgiven for the wrongs he had done. Ian said that he had asked but had not received much of a response.

Before Ian knew what he was saying, he was blurting out before Reverend Emmett the story of his brother's death, then his wife's suicide, telling about the children now under the care of his mother while he was at college, ending with a question to Reverend Emmett.

"Don't you think I'm forgiven?"

"Goodness, no," Reverend Emmett said briskly.

Ian was shaken. Wasn't this the whole point of Christianity? To tell people that God loves them and forgives them?

Reverend Emmett replies, "You can't just say, 'I'm sorry, God.' Why anyone could do that much! You have to offer reparation—concrete, practical reparation, according to the rules of our church."

Suddenly, the matter of forgiveness had become very public, corporate, communal, something to be discussed in public, in worship, in church, something subject to the "rules of our church." And what a church! The Church of the Second Chance uses only first names, feeling that second names endanger linking them to "the world of wealth and connections," people who "came over on the Mayflower," and other corruptions. Furthermore, they all practice the "Sugar Rule," vowing to eat no sugar for some reason which remains rather unclear in the novel.

Ian protests that the bad he has done cannot be undone, repaired. What then? Reverend Emmett cites Jesus, saying that Jesus helps us to undo what can't be undone, only after we have done what we can to make amends. Then he tells Ian directly to "see to those children."

What? A freshman to take on such awesome responsibility? I'm in college, Ian protests. Drop out of college, says Reverend Ian. Give up my education? That would be crazy! I'm nineteen years old! I can't take on a bunch of kids! What kind of stupid religion is this?

"It's the religion of atonement and complete forgiveness," Reverend Emmett says with a peaceful smile. "It's the religion of the Second Chance."

Ian eventually does exactly what Reverend Emmett has so crazily suggested. He drops out of school and adopts the children as his own. No longer able to be a college graduate, Ian becomes a cabinetmaker, principally because that work will give him the time he needs to raise the children.

Ian's mother protests. Their staid, predictable Presbyterian church never asked them to drop out of school, to abandon their way of life.

"Well, maybe it should have," says Ian.

At this point in the novel it is clear that reconciliation to God is not cheap. Many of us say that we would like to be close to God, that we would like to be free of our sin and at peace. But at what price? We want reconciliation, but we also want success, as contemporary culture defines success. In the words of Hazel Motes, anyone with a good car doesn't need redemption.

Freedom from the powers which hold us is not cheap, nor is it easy. It must come from more than simply the inner determination to do better. It comes from specific, concrete, costly acts of commitment and reconciliation. It comes from being bound into a community which holds us accountable, which makes specific demands upon us, which gives us a way out of our enslavement. This, wherever it occurs, is The Church of the Second Chance.

After Ian's fateful decision to drop out of school and raise the children, the novel settles down into a celebration of the joys of the ordinary life of an ordinary family. Ian has no time for romantic relationships. The children consume all of his day. The Church of the Second Chance and Reverend Emmett keep him going, helping with the children, providing Ian the emotional and spiritual support he needs. Fixing meals, enjoying neighbors, watching his parents age, celebrating the growth of the children and their various personalities, provide Ian with a great sense of satisfaction. By the end of the novel, his difficult, oldest adopted daughter proclaims Ian "a saint . . . maybe."

It is the story of a life redeemed, of a terrible tragedy for which Ian is to blame or for which no one is to blame, taken, redeemed, transformed by countless ordinary acts of beauty and goodness. The story suggests that the path toward redemption, our way back to God, is not without cost, without risk and difficult choices. It is a path too demanding to walk alone, therefore it is important that the church not only invites us to walk it but also walks it with us. There is, as the church once proclaimed, "No salvation outside the church." That is, no salvation we know of which is not also communal and corporate. Without the ministrations of The Church of the Second Chance, for all their assorted weirdness, Ian knows he could not have made it.

Saint Maybe may be one of our century's greatest novels about the church. It is the story of Ian, a wonderfully ordinary person who, by the novel's end, has done some absolutely extraordinary things. The children are raised and become interesting, loved, and loving persons. Ian is at peace. He has been redeemed. But this redemption has been wrought through the rather eccentric means of grace named The Church of the Second Chance.

I'm a United Methodist, heir to John Wesley's revival of religion in eighteenth century England. Among Wesley's great contributions to the church was his conviction that it was possible to take utterly ordinary English people and transform them into saints.

A favorite Wesleyan text occurs at the end of Jesus' Sermon on the Mount when Jesus, after urging us to turn the other cheek, not to remarry after divorce, to love our enemies, and other seeming impossibilities, ends by urging us to "be perfect, as your heavenly Father is perfect" (Matthew 5:48). Wesley took this text with absolute seriousness. How is it possible to make people like us perfect? It is not enough to attempt to weasel out of this demanding text by saying something like,

"He didn't really mean *perfect*. He meant something like 'mature,' or 'complete.'"

Well then, how is it possible to make people like us mature or complete?

Wesley knew enough to know that such demand could not have been addressed to the church as he had experienced it. Therefore, rather than attempting to change the text (our usual modern way with the Bible) Wesley sought to change the church, to transform the church into the sort of body whereby ordinary people might be transformed.

Wesley virtually invented the small, covenant group, the group in which we would hold one another accountable in the name of Christ. Any church which sought to make folk "perfect" would be a church where there would be a great deal of failure, much sin. Therefore it must be a church where there is much forgiveness, an abundance of grace. In Wesley's "classes," people were made to feel a part of something larger than themselves; their lives were turned into an adventure. They were made to feel responsibility for someone other than themselves. They got to be priests to one another.

Quite erroneously, the philosopher Whitehead defined religion as "what we do with our solitude." Christians believe, quite to the contrary, that religion is what we do in churches. In our constitutional democracy, we have reduced religion to a personal lifestyle option, something akin to the choice of a hobby or preference for hair-coloring.

We made a mistake, in contemporary Christianity, in falling into this arrangement, in presenting the Christian faith as something personal, private, my own business, a matter of my personal decisions. Personal convictions, privately held, are no match for the principalities and powers. The tragic in life is too vast for us to solve through our pumped-up positive attitudes. Our lives, left to their own devices, tend to be flat without the encouragement and example of the saints. Therefore the primary way of Jesus' dealing with the world is through the community of faith, as a group. It's a Body thing rather than a private thing.

That first night, just after Ian wandered into The Church of the Second Chance, he is shocked when forthrightly asked by Reverend Emmett, "What was it that you needed to be forgiven?"

Ian can't believe his ears. He asks himself, "Was this even legal, inquiring into a person's private prayers?"

Ian is now in the presence of a different way of thinking about the world where there really is no such thing as "private prayers." Our prayer as Christians tends to be very public, even when we do it alone. Our paradigmatic prayer, The Lord's Prayer, is not a way of addressing God which we devised on our own. It is a communal gift. Furthermore, when we pray, we pray, "*Our* Father, who art in heaven . . ."

Is The Church of the Second Chance really so odd, or is it more fair to say that, in a society which abandons its young to their own devices, implying that it is possible for them to think up the significance of their lives on their own, any group of people who adopt, discipline, convict, and forgive, are going to look odd?

One thing the church does for us, when the church is at its best, is to gather up our ordinary little lives into a larger adventure called the Kingdom of God. Small, unspectacular acts of faithfulness, often faithfulness we did not consciously "choose"—like caring for children or nursing an aging parent—are named as discipleship, following Jesus. Jesus invites us to take up our cross and to follow him daily. In the daily, ordinary responsibilities on behalf of others—particularly on behalf of the very young, the very old, the very vulnerable of any age—our work is redeemed, sanctified as holy work.

Many modern people are frustrated in their relationship to God. They have gotten the erroneous impression that Christianity is something they are supposed to feel in their hearts, some inner disposition of the soul. Inner dispositions and feelings are notoriously fickle and difficult to sustain over the long haul. Aristotle said that it was too much to expect ordinary folk, folk like us, to be good. About the best that one could do with ordinary people was to teach us good habits. We need external, habitual disciplines which keep us at discipleship even when we don't feel like it.

John Wesley's people were ridiculed as "Methodists" because they believed that some matters, particularly matters of discipleship, were too important to be left up to chance. Therefore they gave ordinary people methods, disciplines to keep them at it. Grace is, in this view, not that which frees us from all method and discipline but rather those gifts of God which arise from following the method and being true to the discipline. Ian certainly discovers grace, but not as some inner feeling. Rather, grace arises as a gift of his being faithful to the needs of the children under his care. His life is thereby given shape and significance it would not have had if he had not conformed his life to something more significant than his own desires.

So Ian gets enlisted to be part of a movement of greater significance than his own life project. He is adopted, taken in among the baptized, engrafted into a family with a considerably larger memory, and with far greater resources, than his natural family. Redemption comes through The Church of the Second Chance and its determination to make Ian more than he would have been if he had been left to his own devices. This is how redemption in the name of Jesus occurs. This is how saints are made.

Maybe.

For Further Reflection

1. What are the specific, practical, ordinary spiritual disciplines which you follow in your life which are redemptive?

2. Are there ways in which you are bending your life toward God and away from your own selfish desires?

3. Take a moment and list the ways in which the church has given you gifts which you could not have had if you had been left to your own devices.

10

A
God-Haunted
World

Mariette in Ecstasy

When the day of Pentecost had come, they were all
together in one place. And suddenly from heaven there
came the sound like the rush of a violent wind.
—Acts 2:1-2

In her book *The Greek Way,* Edith Hamilton writes that the temple priests of ancient Greece had a stake in fostering a fear of mystery. Priests of every age, says Hamilton, feed on humanity's awe of the mysterious. Priests always deprecate humanity's attempt rationally to unravel mystery and thereby to learn more about reality.

But might the case be that mystery is a part of life? Mystery is not something dreamed up by priests to keep people under their power; mystery bubbles up in your life and mine quite naturally. What if the mysterious is not a restraint in our quest for the real, but an essential quality in what is real? From this perspective, priests may be among the only leaders of society with the guts to talk about what the rest of us are trained to avoid. Of course, I am a priest, so perhaps I can't be trusted on matters of mystery.

"At last I know what I'm supposed to do," he said to me. "At last I know what God wants me to do with my life."

I received this declaration with more than a little interest. Having logged at least four or five hours with him, hashing out the question of what he ought to do after graduation, I was pleased that he had at last come to a decision. But how had he come to clarity?

"Well you might ask," he said. "I was driving home from work a couple of days ago, turning over in my mind the pros and the cons of going into elementary teaching. Traffic had come to a stop. I looked over to the left. There was this billboard, partially covered by a tree. The only word I could make out on the billboard was 'GO.' Just that. 'GO.'

"Traffic began moving. I drove about another mile. Traffic stopped. I looked at a torn bumper sticker on the car in front of mine. Most of the bumper sticker was gone except for letters which spelled, 'NOW.' Can you believe that? 'NOW.' Well, of course I knew what I had to do."

"What?" I responded in astonishment. "That's a tree in front of a billboard. A torn bumper sticker. You're going to base your life on that?"

Somewhat hurt he said, "Well, I guess you'd have had to have been there. It sure seemed like the voice of God to me."

Of course, in evaluating whether or not this young man is crazy to take such events as signs, as divine communication, one would have to inquire into what sort of world we live in. Do we live in a world where God lives, where God intrudes, acts, moves, speaks? If we answer that we do not live in such a world, then the young man's reading of the data is bizarre at best, insane at worst. However, if we live in a place where revelation is possible, then . . .

Each of us is living life on the basis of some conviction about the world. "Reality" is that name we give to our picture of the world. Our definition of reality enables us to see certain things going on in the world and to ignore others. John Calvin spoke of Scripture as the "lens" through which we look at the world. Reading the Bible is like putting on a pair of spectacles whereby certain things come into focus which we had not seen before, and other things are pushed out of focus. We can't see everything at once. We can't give equal valence to everything that goes on "out there" and "in here." Modern North American people may be living in a rather narrowly defined world, a world where only a limited range of data is admitted into view, a world which is flat.

In J. B. Priestley's autobiographical novel, *Midnight on the Desert*, he recalls reading a strange novel, *Flatland* which was published in England in the late nineteenth century. *Flatland* is a story about a world which is flat, everything in two dimensions. The chief character in the novel is Mr. Square, who is, of course, only in two dimensions.

One day, Mr. Square is visited by a Mr. Sphere who is, of necessity, in three dimensions. Square regards Sphere quite apprehensively. Sphere speaks to Square about a world of three dimensions, a world which is not flat. But Square is unconvinced. Living in a two-dimensional world makes it impossible for him to imagine another dimension. Eventually, Sphere is persecuted and driven out by the outraged Flatlanders.

John Killinger says that we are Flatlanders. We live in a world of two dimensions, unable to grasp the possibility of a reality beyond that which we have experienced. We are modern, Western folk who have taught ourselves to be content with a flat, well-defined, and utterly accessible world. Our world has become "user friendly," for we can imagine no world worth having which is not subject to our utility. Our ways of knowing are positivistic, historicist, and inherently reductionistic.

It is of the nature of modernity to be arrogant, to believe that we are the first people in the history of the world to disbelieve, to be critical and skeptical. We stand in sovereign judgment upon everyone and everything which preceded us. Therefore, certain data are excluded from our purview. Ironically, the modern world thinks of itself as open, broad-minded, enjoying unlimited vistas when, in reality, it is a very closed, narrow way of living and looking. Many modern people have therefore come to believe that, in modernity, our world did not grow, as was promised. Rather, it shrunk.

Robert Alter says somewhere that, until the parables of Kafka or James Joyce's *Ulysses*, there is a sense in which we modern people had lost the skills necessary to read the Bible. Only after artists were again determined to write reality on a number of levels, exploring the complexities of human consciousness, the mystery of time, the polyvalence of words, were we able to ask the right questions of First Kings. The Bible demands of us a wider consciousness.

Mariette in Ecstasy seems to me a postmodern novel. Ron Hansen seems intent on exploring areas of human consciousness and experience that we have for some time denied. Here, in poetic, simply eloquent style, is an unprejudiced look at a world which is mystifying, surprising, where God may appear.

We are in a convent in upstate New York in the early 1900s. One part of upstate New York earned the designation as "The Burned Over District" for all of the religious outbreaks which occurred in a relatively small geographical area in the nineteenth century. Surely this convent is in that same area.

The novel begins with a listing of the names and ages of the sisters in residence at "Our Lady of the Afflictions." A young woman, aged seventeen, named Mariette Baptiste, is received into the convent as a postulant among these Sisters of the Crucifixion. Within a few pages, we are enticed into the world of the convent, the daily duties of the Sisters, their round of prayer and praise, the quiet, deceptively quiet life in their tight little world.

It is a small world inside the convent, yet from the first the reader has the impression that it is a strange, wonderful, mysterious, perhaps even menacing world where the Sisters tiptoe upon a thin crust, where underneath, something lies just waiting to break forth.

The convent is portrayed as a little fort where the nuns go about their business, but outside, lying in wait, in the surrounding countryside, things are alive, throbbing, waiting as if ready to pounce. Each chapter opens with recognition of the world surrounding the convent, with nature, strange, haunted by some significance deeper than the apparent:

Half-moon and a wrack of gray clouds.
Church windows and thirty nuns singing the
Night Office in Gregorian chant. Matins. Lauds. And
then silence.
    Wind, and a nighthawk teetering on it and yaw-
ing away into woods.

Many have noted the "disenchantment" of the world which
occurred as a byproduct of the scientific world view. All that was
left, after we pried open the lid and stared into the mysterious
dark, was a flat, cause-and-effect, well-explained universe.
Hansen portrays a different world. Gradually, he draws us into a
mystical world where we are willing to be enchanted.

D. H. Lawrence, romantic rebel against modern disenchantment, urged us to become "un-tamed" by "listening-in to the
voices of the honorable beasts that call in the dark paths of the
veins of our body, from the God in the heart. Listening inwards,
inwards, not for words nor for inspiration, but to the lowing of
the innermost beasts, the feelings that roam in the forest of the
blood, from the feet of God within the red, dark heart."[1]

Of course, the pagan Lawrence was speaking of the "God
within" whereas Hansen is depicting a God who intrudes into
the world which God has created. No limp extension of ourselves, this God hovers, hides, entices, seduces, embraces us. We
know, shortly into the novel, that there will be some sort of
encounter with this God.

Something is about to happen to Mariette and her sisters,
though we don't know what. There is something foreboding
about the convent and its inhabitants, something mysterious,
sensual, almost erotic, menacing. Here are women who have run
away to God, who have no lover and want none except the
Christ.

1. E. D. McDonald, ed., *The Novel and Feelings*. Quoted in *Phoenix: The Posthu-
mous Papers of D. H. Lawrence* (New York: The Viking Press, 1936), pp. 755-759.

Mariette is being examined by someone, a church official. The book is in part her response to his questions. Something has happened. What? Life in the convent is described in first person, then third person, and always outside is a world throbbing, waiting, alive with life which cannot be contained, defined, or simply understood.

When, one day at work, as she scrubs the floor, blood begins to drip from holes in each of Mariette's hands, we are not surprised. We have been expecting something, not this perhaps, but something. We knew that something was afoot in the convent, some mystery just waiting to show itself before us. "Oh, look at what Jesus has done to me!" Mariette exclaims, holding her "blood-painted hands like a present" before the convent's old priest. Mariette has received the stigmata, the marks of the crucified Christ.

The reaction of the Mother Superior, the priest, and the others is rather predictable. They are skeptical, incredulous. Odd that religious people, particularly the professionally religious, should be thought of as gullible, credulous, when we tend to be the most skeptical of all that there has been some strange divine intrusion among us. In examining her wounds, Sister Aimee cannot hide her contempt for the silly young girl:

"Is it deep?" the priest asks.

"Christ's was deeper," sister Aimee says.

Some of the nuns are excited, others are envious, some are downright hostile to Mariette. It is clear that, to those in charge of the convent, Mariette's experience is an unwelcomed event. Things become disordered, difficult. Their tranquil life together has been disrupted and most of them know not what to make of it all. One night Mariette awakes to the sound of someone in her cell, head rustling under her bedclothes in the darkness. The intruder disappears. She thinks to herself that she was dreaming. Then she realizes she is not. Dreaming or awake, the line between what is real and what is not, even the very definition of something fixed as "real," is being dismantled before us.

Eventually, Mariette is forced to leave the convent. We are not surprised. Folk on the threshold of the twentieth century do not do well with such phenomena. Perhaps religious, church folk, have particular difficulty with the mysterious.

I read *Mariette in Ecstasy* at one sitting. By the time I laid the finished book aside, I knew that it had not finished with me. I walked out into a gently snowy Minnesota evening and realized that my world had been freshly re-enchanted, haunted once again by spirits, perhaps The Spirit, which I had so conventionally excluded.

I was changed. My previously rather self-confident "Modern World," which I had taken with such seriousness, now seemed less substantial, in crisis, dismantled, dislodged by a book.

Shortly thereafter, I read Annie Dillard's wonderful autobiography where she told of her childhood discovery of the power of fiction. What adults seemed to treat as a harmless, healthy pastime, Dillard discovered to be dynamite:

> I had been driven into nonfiction against my wishes. I wanted to read fiction, but I had learned to be cautious about it.
>
> "When you open a book," the sentimental library posters said, "anything can happen." This was so. A book of fiction was a bomb. It was a land mine you wanted to go off. You wanted it to blow your whole day. Unfortunately, hundreds of thousands of books were duds. They had been rusting out of everyone's way for so long that they no longer worked. There was no way to distinguish the duds from the live mines except to throw yourself at them headlong, one by one."[2]

For me, in my rather self-contained, secure, modern existence, *Mariette in Ecstasy* was a bomb, a mind-blowing, world-

2. Annie Dillard, *An American Childhood* (Harper & Row: New York, 1987), p. 97.

shattering, wonderful bomb. Smug, modern people living in our flatlandish existence yearn for such explosiveness, for God to come to us and blow open the closed doors of our mind.

The experience which Hansen so poetically, subtly portrays in *Mariette in Ecstasy* is similar to that reported in Acts 2.

"When the day of Pentecost had come, they were all together in one place. And suddenly from heaven there came a sound like the rush of a violent wind" (Acts 2:1-2).

It is this earth-shattering, shaking, piercing intrusion of the Holy Spirit for which we yearn, even when we do not know for what we yearn.

For Further Reflection

1. One reason why people read books like this one is to explore the mysterious, the divine. In what way is this exploration as much a threat to you as a benefit?

2. What are the ways in which we exclude the mysterious and the transcendent from our lives?